Editorial

Proliferate Peace

Daily, or so it seems, US Air Force B52 strategic bombers depart their base at Fairford in southern England, usually in pairs, to fly missions across Europe, over the Middle East and, occasionally, the Mediterranean Sea and North Africa. These ancient warhorses pollute the atmosphere, burning vast quantities of fuel, to show the flag and test the enemy. Some of them are nuclear capable, some not: a physical modification signals which. We are regularly told that no nuclear weapons are carried on such missions.

Recently, a nuclear capable B52 flew close to the Russian border with Estonia. Indeed, the B52s now spend much time in the skies over the Baltics and Scandinavia, as Finland and Sweden integrate more fully with the nuclear-armed North Atlantic Treaty Organization. Conspicuous nuclear provocation, initially reduced when President Biden succeeded Donald Trump, is back with us following President Putin's criminal invasion of Ukraine accompanied by his threats of 'swift, lightning fast' responses to 'unacceptable strategic threats' (see *Spokesman 151*). One threat begets another. And, as war rages in eastern Ukraine, Russian bloggers call for 'pre-emptive nuclear strikes'.

In this unpropitious context in August 2022, the long delayed tenth review conference of the Nuclear Non-Proliferation Treaty met at the United Nations in New York. We print UN Secretary-General António Guterres' opening remarks about the urgency of reducing the 'nuclear danger', which he emphasised days later by travelling from New York to Hiroshima to commemorate the atomic bombing of that city 77 years ago. The Secretary-General then remained hopeful that the NPT review conference would agree a way forward on reducing the nuclear threat. He cautioned delegates that 'humanity is in danger of forgetting the lessons forged in the terrifying fires of Hiroshima and Nagasaki'. But President Putin and others turned a deaf ear to the Secretary-General and no consensual way forward could be agreed.

Whilst in Hiroshima on 6 August, the Secretary-General told his audience that 'members of the Treaty on the Prohibition of Nuclear Weapons met for the first time to develop a roadmap towards a world free of these doomsday weapons'. We print the political declaration and roadmap of this pioneering inaugural conference, which met in Vienna in June. The nuclear-armed states had previously united in their opposition to the TPNW, and some NATO members attended as observers in Vienna. Recognition of internationally agreed nuclear-weapons-free zones, and guarantees against nuclear threats against such zones on the part of nuclear-armed states, form central signposts on the roadmap.

As the Secretary-General said in Japan, 'it's time to proliferate peace'.

* * *

Bruce Kent was an avid reader of *The Spokesman* journal, judging by the feedback we regularly received from him. On 18 May 2022 in London, he joined us in raising a glass to Bertrand Russell, whose 150th birthday we were celebrating at Conway Hall. So it came as a great shock, a few weeks later, to hear of Bruce's death. In his own inimitable style, Bruce contributed book reviews to *The Spokesman* over the decades, which afford some sense of the man himself. He is greatly missed.

As this year sees Kurt Vonnegut's centenary, we also revisit his timeless address, *Fates Worse than Death*, which he sent to Ken Coates of the Russell Foundation in lieu of travelling to Brussels for the first European Nuclear Disarmament Convention in Brussels in 1982.

Bruce and Kurt were surely kindred spirits in speaking out for peace.

Tony Simpson

The Spokesman
Proliferate Peace
Edited by Tony Simpson and Tom Unterrainer

Published by Spokesman for the
Bertrand Russell Peace Foundation
Ken Coates: Editor 1970 to 2010

Spokesman 152 — 2022

Subscriptions
Institutions £40.00 (ex UK)
£33.00 (UK)
Individuals £20.00 (UK)
£25.00 (ex UK)

A CIP catalogue record for this book is available from the British Library

Published by
The Bertrand Russell Peace Foundation Ltd,
5 Churchill Park,
Nottingham, NG4 2HF
England
Tel. 0115 9708318
email: editor@russfound.org
www.spokesmanbooks.org
www.russfound.org

Editorial Board
John Daniels
Kate Fleet
Stuart Holland
Henry McCubbin
Abi Rhodes
Regan Scott

CONTENTS

Editorial	3	
No More Hiroshimas! No More Nagasakis!	5	António Guterres
"Our Commitment to a World Free of Nuclear Weapons"	11	States Parties to the TPNW
Plain Speaking	27	Bruce Kent
Riding Two Horses	48	Glyn Ford
Appointment in Wales	52	Tony Simpson, Richard Fletcher
Workers' Plans	58	Mike George
Fates worse than Death	68	Kurt Vonnegut
Making Palestine's History	81	Jehan Helou
Eyewitness in Beirut	85	Tony Simpson
Soldiers 2	89	Ben Thompson
Reviews	90	Barry Baldwin, Nathan Collett, Sharen Green
END Info	103	Tom Unterrainer, Annika Strandhäll, Helena Cobban, David Barash, Cynthia Lazaroff, Richard Falk, Tim Street

Cover: UN Secretary-General in Hiroshima, 6 August 2022

ISSN 1367 7748   ISBN 978 0 85124 9131

BERTRAND RUSSELL

Recent titles from Spokesman Books

BERTRAND RUSSELL, *A LIFE*
by Caroline Moorehead

This new edition of Caroline Moorehead's acclaimed biography is published to mark the 150th anniversary year of Bertrand Russell's birth in 1872.

632 pages | ISBN 978 0 85124 9018 | £19.99

BERTRAND RUSSELL, *PUBLIC INTELLECTUAL*
Edited by Timothy Madigan and Peter Stone

A wide-ranging and highly accessible anthology whose ambit is actually considerably wider than its title would suggest.

342 pages | ISBN 978 0 85124 9100 | £19.99

TO BE FRANK: *The Politics and Polemics of a Radical Russell*
Ruth Derham

The 2nd Earl Russell, John Francis Stanley, described himself as a socialist and strong individualist, but primarily innately rebellious.

210 pages | ISBN 978 0 85124 9117 | £16.99

BERTRAND RUSSELL 150 (*The Spokesman 150*)
Edited by Tony Simpson and Tom Unterrainer

The Spokesman marks its 150th edition with a celebration of Russell's 150th anniversary.

150 pages | ISBN 978 0 85124 9049 | £6

www.spokesmanbooks.org

No more Hiroshimas! No more Nagasakis!

António Guterres

The Secretary-General of the United Nations opened the tenth review conference of the parties to the Treaty on Non-Proliferation of Nuclear Weapons in New York on 1 August 2022, chaired by Ambassador Zlauvinen of Argentina. Five days later, on 6 August, Mr Guterres spoke in Hiroshima at the commemoration of the atomic bombing of the city in 1945. Later, he was given honorary citizenship of the city.

New York

… This Conference has been long-delayed. But its importance and urgency remain undiminished. It takes place at a critical juncture for our collective peace and security. The climate crisis, stark inequalities, conflicts and human rights violations, and the personal and economic devastation caused by the COVID-19 pandemic, have put our world under greater stress than it has faced in our lifetimes. And it occurs at a time of nuclear danger not seen since the height of the Cold War. That is the reason that to underscore the importance of this conference, I will be in a few days in Hiroshima at the anniversary of the first nuclear bombardment in human history. And then, I will follow it with two visits to other countries in the region having non-proliferation as a key item in the agenda of the visits.

Now, the initial post-Cold War period ushered in a tentative new hope for peace: a hope found in massive arsenal reductions, in entire regions declaring themselves to be nuclear-weapons-free, and in the entrenchment of norms against the use, proliferation and testing of nuclear weapons. When I was Prime Minister of Portugal, I instructed our mission to the United Nations to vote – for the first time – against the resumption of nuclear testing in the Pacific. Before, the tradition of my country was to abstain, as if this was a matter in which we can abstain. And through a combination of commitment, judgment and luck, the world avoided the suicidal mistake of nuclear conflict. But as the years have passed, these fruits of hope are withering. Humanity is in danger of forgetting the lessons forged in the terrifying fires of Hiroshima and Nagasaki.

Geopolitical tensions are reaching new highs. Competition is trumping co-operation and collaboration. Distrust has replaced dialogue and disunity has replaced disarmament. States are seeking false security in stockpiling and spending hundreds of billions of dollars on doomsday weapons that have no place on our planet. Almost 13,000 nuclear weapons are now being held in arsenals around the world. All this at a time when the risks of proliferation are growing and guardrails to prevent escalation are weakening. And when crises – with nuclear undertones – are festering. From the Middle East and the Korean Peninsula; to the invasion of Ukraine by Russia, and to many other factors around the world.

The clouds that parted following the end of the Cold War are gathering once more. We have been extraordinarily lucky so far. But luck is not a strategy. Nor is it a shield from geopolitical tensions boiling over into nuclear conflict. Today, humanity is just one misunderstanding, one miscalculation away from nuclear annihilation. We need the Treaty on Non-Proliferation of Nuclear Weapons as much as ever. That is why this Review Conference is so important. It's an opportunity to hammer out the measures that will help avoid certain disaster; and to put humanity on a new path towards a world free of nuclear weapons. It's also a chance to strengthen this Treaty and make it fit for the worrying world around us.

I suggest five areas for action.

First – we urgently need to reinforce and reaffirm the 77-year-old norm against the use of nuclear weapons. This requires a steadfast commitment from all States Parties. It means finding practical measures that will reduce the risk of nuclear war and put us back on the path to disarmament. We need to strengthen all avenues of dialogue and transparency. Peace cannot take hold in an absence of trust and mutual respect.

Second – reducing the risk of war is not enough. Eliminating nuclear weapons is the only guarantee they will never be used. We must work relentlessly towards this goal. This must start with new commitments to shrink the numbers of all kinds of nuclear weapons so that they no longer hang by a thread over humanity. And it means reinvigorating – and fully resourcing – our multilateral agreements and frameworks around disarmament and non-proliferation, including the important work of the International Atomic Energy Agency.

Third – we need to address the simmering tensions in the Middle East and Asia. By adding the threat of nuclear weapons to enduring conflicts, these regions are edging towards catastrophe. We need to redouble our support for dialogue and negotiation to ease tensions and forge new bonds of trust in regions that have seen too little.

Fourth – we need to promote the peaceful use of nuclear technology as a catalyst to advance the Sustainable Development Goals, including for medical and other uses. When used for peaceful purposes, this technology can be a great benefit to humanity.

And fifth – we need to fulfil all outstanding commitments in the Treaty itself, and keep it fit-for-purpose in these trying times. We are all here today because we believe in the Treaty's purpose and function. But carrying it into the future requires going beyond the status quo. It requires renewed commitment, and real, good faith negotiations. And it requires all Parties to listen, compromise and keep the lessons of the past – and the fragility of the future – in view at all times.

Future generations are counting on your commitment to step back from the abyss. We have a shared obligation to leave the world a better, safer place than we found it. This is our moment to meet this basic test, and lift the cloud of nuclear annihilation, once and for all.

Hiroshima

… Seventy-seven years ago, tens of thousands of people were killed in this city, in the blink of an eye. Women, children and men were incinerated in a hellish fire. Buildings turned to dust. Survivors were cursed with a radioactive legacy. Polluted by cancer. Stalked by health problems. And marked by telltale scars on their bodies – the stigma of surviving the most destructive attack in human history.

The unflinching testimonies of the *hibakusha* remind us of the fundamental folly of nuclear weapons. Nuclear weapons are nonsense. Three-quarters of a century later, we must ask what we've learned from the mushroom cloud that swelled above this city in 1945. Or from the Cold War and the terrifying near-misses that placed humanity within minutes of annihilation. Or from the promising decades of arsenal reductions and widespread acceptance of the principles against the use, proliferation and testing of nuclear weapons.

Because a new arms race is picking up speed. World leaders are enhancing stockpiles at a cost of hundreds of billions of dollars. Almost 13,000 nuclear weapons are held in arsenals around the world. And crises with grave nuclear undertones are spreading fast – from the Middle East, to the Korean peninsula, to Russia's invasion of Ukraine. It is totally unacceptable for states in possession of nuclear weapons to admit the possibility of nuclear war. Humanity is playing with a loaded gun.

There are signs of hope. In June, members of the Treaty on the Prohibition of Nuclear Weapons met for the first time to develop a roadmap towards a world free of these doomsday weapons. And right now, the Tenth Review Conference of the Treaty on the Non-Proliferation of Nuclear Weapons is taking place in New York. Today, from this sacred space, I call on this Treaty's members to work urgently to eliminate the stockpiles that threaten our future. To strengthen dialogue, diplomacy and negotiation. And to support my disarmament agenda by eliminating these devices of destruction.

Countries with nuclear weapons must commit to the "no first use" of those weapons. They must also assure States that do not have nuclear weapons that they will not use – or threaten to use – nuclear weapons against them. And they must be transparent throughout.

We must keep the horrors of Hiroshima in view at all times, recognizing there is only one solution to the nuclear threat: not to have nuclear weapons at all. At the height of the Cold War, schoolchildren learned to hide under desks. But leaders cannot hide from their responsibilities. My message to them is simple:

Take the nuclear option off the table – for good.
It's time to proliferate peace.

Heed the message of the *hibakusha*:
'No more Hiroshimas! No more Nagasakis!'

And to the young people here today: finish the work that the *hibakusha* have begun. The world must never forget what happened here. The memory of those who died – and the legacy of those who survived – will never be extinguished.

* * *

From horror to hope

Mayor Matsui, City Council Chairperson Sasaki, Ladies and gentlemen, I am deeply moved by this granting of honorary citizenship of Hiroshima. This beautiful and vibrant city epitomizes the necessity of peace. And how people can work together and move from horror to hope. I accept this great honour on behalf of all the women and men of the United Nations who are working for peace around the world. I accept it on behalf of the diplomats and negotiators who – this very week – are meeting in New York to stop the spread of nuclear weapons. I accept it on behalf of the activists – young and old – who continue to stand up and speak out on this issue. I accept it on behalf of the inspiring *hibakusha* I met earlier today who have spent their lives reminding the world of the importance of peace.

Above all, I accept it in the memory of those tens of thousands of people who were killed in Hiroshima and Nagasaki 77 years ago. We must never forget what happened here. Nor can we forget all the victims of global conflicts like World War Two, which inflicted incalculable damage to communities, countries and the world. Especially today, when nuclear risk is once again growing around the world. When stockpiles are being upgraded. And when almost 13,000 of these doomsday weapons still exist.

The lessons of Hiroshima and Nagasaki are clear. Nuclear weapons have no place on our planet. It's time to lift the cloud of nuclear annihilation, once and for all. It's time to proliferate peace.

My thanks to the people of Hiroshima for this honour today. And to the government and people of Japan for your warm welcome and steadfast commitment to a more peaceful future.

And allow me two personal notes. One to say that it is true that we see a new arms race. It is true that disarmament treaties, that disarmament agreements that were made in the last century are at risk and some of them have been lost, but the Conference on the Review of the Non-proliferation Treaty is going well and I hope that there will be positive outcomes and the States party to the Treaty on Prohibition of Nuclear Weapons are working to define a roadmap with relation to the progressive implementation of the Treaty. So I see movement in the right direction. I think Hiroshima has a key role to play in helping us to move in the right direction and I was very impressed by the declaration of peace that you, honourable mayor, have made today.

The second note, I came to Hiroshima, I think 39 years ago. I visited the city and I visited the area at the Peace Memorial and I visited the museum – it was a small museum at the time – but it was very impressive and this made a very deep imprint in myself. Then, I became Prime Minister of Portugal and just one month after starting functions, there was a vote in the General Assembly of the United Nations about the French nuclear tests in the Pacific. France had announced the tests. There was a motion as every year, a proposal for a resolution against the test. Now, the Minister for Foreign Affairs called me and said, well we have this resolution and the tradition is that all the members of the European Union will abstain so as not to offend France. But at that moment, I remembered my visit to Hiroshima and I told the Minister: Sorry, we are going to vote against, which means we vote in favour of the resolution which is against the explosion.

And so this is very complicated because other ambassadors already promised the French that they would abstain as always. I said it doesn't matter, we vote against the nuclear explosion. Afterwards two other European countries, I think Austria and another one, when they knew that Portugal was going to vote against, they also voted against.

We'd probably keep on with this abstention if I had not come to Hiroshima. So it's impossible for people to come here and not to feel the absurdity of the existence of nuclear weapons. And I join my voice for Heads of State of all over the world to come here to understand that we must have a world free of nuclear weapons.

... The current context also gives us pause to consider the devastating humanitarian consequences of nuclear weapons. Any use of nuclear weapons would have immediate and long-term consequences, creating a devastating humanitarian crisis and emergency significantly beyond the response capacity of States or international organisations. I welcome the adoption of the Vienna Declaration of the Treaty on the Prohibition of Nuclear Weapons, which sends a clear message of alarm and dismay at threats to use nuclear weapons, and unequivocally condemns "any and all nuclear threats, whether they be explicit or implicit and irrespective of the circumstances." The outcome of the Vienna meeting successfully demonstrated the value of the TPNW for its States parties as a pathway to fulfilling Article VI obligations. The TPNW is fully compatible with and complements the NPT. We hope to see the positive contribution of the TPNW reflected in the outcome document of this meeting ...

Ireland's National Statement at the 10th NPT Review Conference

"Our Commitment to a World Free of Nuclear Weapons"

The historic first Meeting of States Parties to the Treaty on the Prohibition of Nuclear Weapons concluded in Vienna on 23 June 2022. It adopted a political declaration and practical action plan that set the course for the implementation of the Treaty and progress towards its goal of the total elimination of nuclear weapons.

Draft Vienna Declaration of the 1st Meeting of States Parties of the Treaty on the Prohibition of Nuclear Weapons

1. We, the States Parties to the Treaty on the Prohibition of Nuclear Weapons, have gathered here for the first Meeting of States Parties, to mark the Treaty's entry into force, to reaffirm our determination to realize the complete elimination of nuclear weapons and to chart our path forward for the full and effective implementation of the Treaty. We welcome the broad participation of signatory states and observers, as well as other observers, civil society representatives and survivors of nuclear weapons use and testing.

2. We celebrate the entry into force of the Treaty on 22 January 2021. Nuclear weapons are now explicitly and comprehensively prohibited by international law, as has long been the case for biological and chemical weapons. We welcome that the Treaty fills this gap in the international legal regime against weapons of mass destruction and reaffirm the need for all states to comply at all times with applicable international law, including international humanitarian law.

3. We reiterate the moral and ethical imperatives which inspired and motivated the creation of the Treaty and which now drive and guide its implementation:
- That the establishment of a legally binding prohibition on nuclear weapons constitutes a fundamental step towards the irreversible, verifiable and transparent elimination of nuclear weapons needed for the achievement and maintenance of a

world free of nuclear weapons and, hence, for the realization of the purposes and principles of the Charter of the United Nations.
• That the catastrophic humanitarian consequences of nuclear weapons cannot be adequately addressed, transcend national borders, pose grave implications for human survival and well-being and are incompatible with respect for the right to life. They inflict destruction, death and displacement, as well as profound long-term damage to the environment, socioeconomic and sustainable development, the global economy, food security and the health of current and future generations, including with regard to the disproportionate impacts they have on women and girls.
• That all states share the responsibility to achieve nuclear disarmament, to prevent the proliferation of nuclear weapons in all its aspects, to prevent any use or threat of use of nuclear weapons and, to assist victims, redress the harms and remediate the environmental damage caused by previous use and testing of nuclear armed states in accordance with their respective obligations under international law and bilateral agreements.
• That the risk of a nuclear weapon detonation by accident, miscalculation or design concerns the security of all humanity and achieving and maintaining a nuclear-weapon-free world serves both national and collective security interests.
• That the risks posed to all humanity by the existence of nuclear weapons are, thus, so grave that immediate action is needed to achieve a world without nuclear weapons. This is the only way to guarantee that they are never used again, under any circumstances. We cannot afford to wait.

4. We are alarmed and dismayed by threats to use nuclear weapons and increasingly strident nuclear rhetoric. We stress that any use or threat of use of nuclear weapons is a violation of international law, including the Charter of the United Nations. We condemn unequivocally any and all nuclear threats, whether they be explicit or implicit and irrespective of the circumstances.

5. Far from preserving peace and security, nuclear weapons are used as instruments of policy, linked to coercion, intimidation and heightening of tensions. This highlights now more than ever the fallacy of nuclear deterrence doctrines, which are based and rely on the threat of the actual use of nuclear weapons and, hence, the risks of the destruction of countless

lives, of societies, of nations, and of inflicting global catastrophic consequences. We thus insist that, pending the total elimination of nuclear weapons, all nuclear-armed states never use or threaten to use these weapons under any circumstances.

6. We remain gravely concerned that nine states still possess between them approximately 13,000 nuclear weapons and by security doctrines, which set out rationales for the use or threat of use of nuclear weapons. Many of these weapons are on high alert and ready to be launched within minutes. We are further concerned that some non-nuclear armed states continue to advocate for nuclear deterrence and encourage the ongoing possession of nuclear weapons. Growing instability and outright conflict greatly exacerbate the risks that these weapons will be used, whether deliberately or by accident or miscalculation. The existence of nuclear weapons diminishes and threatens the common security of all states; indeed, it threatens our very survival.

7. We regret and are deeply concerned that despite the terrible risks, and despite their legal obligations and political commitments to disarm, none of the nuclear-armed states and their allies under the nuclear umbrella are taking any serious steps to reduce their reliance on nuclear weapons. Instead, all nuclear-armed states are spending vast sums to maintain, modernize, upgrade or expand their nuclear arsenals and are placing a greater emphasis on and increasing the role of nuclear weapons in security doctrines. We strongly call for an immediate end to these disconcerting trends. We underscore that these resources could be better utilized for sustainable development.

8. In these circumstances, the Treaty on the Prohibition of Nuclear Weapons is needed more than ever. We will move forward with its implementation, with the aim of further stigmatizing and de-legitimizing nuclear weapons and steadily building a robust global peremptory norm against them.

9. Together, we are developing the mechanisms of the Treaty. We will discharge our national obligations in full. We will work in partnership with the United Nations, the International Red Cross and Red Crescent Movement, other international and regional organizations, the International Campaign to Abolish Nuclear Weapons and other non-governmental organizations, religious leaders, parliamentarians,

academics, indigenous peoples, victims of the use of nuclear weapons (hibakusha), as well as those affected by nuclear testing and youth groups. We recognize and appreciate their valuable contribution to taking forward nuclear disarmament. We will continue to draw on the expertise of leading scientists and consult and work inclusively with affected communities.

10. The Treaty's humanitarian spirit is reflected in its positive obligations, aimed at redressing the harm caused by nuclear weapons use and testing. We will strengthen international cooperation amongst States Parties to advance the implementation of the positive obligations of this Treaty. We will work with affected communities to provide age and gender sensitive assistance without discrimination to survivors of use or testing of nuclear weapons, and to remediate environmental contamination. We emphasize the innovative gender provisions of the Treaty and stress the importance of the equal, full and effective participation of both women and men in nuclear disarmament diplomacy.

11. We will work to build the membership of the Treaty in all regions. We will harness the public conscience in support of our goal of universal adherence to the Treaty and its full implementation. We will work to implement the Action Plan that we have adopted to guide our efforts to achieve the Treaty's objectives and goals. We will meet regularly to review the implementation of this Treaty and we will identify any additional measures to strengthen the Treaty and move nuclear disarmament forward.

12. We will also work with states outside the Treaty. We recognize the Treaty on the Non-Proliferation of Nuclear Weapons (NPT) as the cornerstone of the disarmament and nonproliferation regime, and deplore threats or actions that risk undermining it. As fully committed states parties to the NPT, we reaffirm the complementarity of the Treaty with the NPT. We are pleased to have advanced the implementation of the NPT's Article VI by bringing into force a comprehensive legal prohibition of nuclear weapons, as a necessary and effective measure related to the cessation of the nuclear arms race and to nuclear disarmament. We urge all NPT States Parties to reinvigorate their efforts to fully implement the obligation of Article VI and the actions and commitments agreed at NPT review conferences. We reiterate our commitment to work constructively with all NPT States Parties to achieve our shared objectives.

13. We will continue to support all measures that can effectively contribute

to nuclear disarmament. These include efforts to bring into force the Comprehensive Nuclear-Test-Ban Treaty, interim measures to reduce the risk of use and threat of use of nuclear weapons, further development of disarmament verification measures, strengthening negative security assurances and a legal instrument prohibiting fissile material for the production for nuclear weapons and other nuclear explosive devices. We pledge to continue collaborating with Nuclear Weapons Free Zones, affirming that the prohibitions, obligations and objectives of the Treaty on the Prohibition of Nuclear Weapons are fully compatible with and complementary to the treaties establishing these Zones.

14. We pledge to highlight further the urgency of nuclear disarmament, the important evidence regarding the humanitarian consequences and risks posed by the existence of nuclear weapons in all relevant disarmament and non-proliferation processes and to the global public more widely. The prevention of these consequences must be at the centre of our collective efforts to achieve and maintain a world without these weapons.

15. We urge all states to join the Treaty on the Prohibition of Nuclear Weapons without delay. We appeal to those states that are not yet ready to take this step to engage cooperatively with the Treaty and work with us in support of our shared goal of a world free of nuclear weapons. We deplore the actions of some nuclear-armed states to discourage non-nuclear-armed states from joining the Treaty. We suggest that the energy and resources of these states would be better directed to making concrete progress towards nuclear disarmament. This would truly contribute to sustainable peace, security and development for all. We would welcome and celebrate such progress.

16. We have no illusions about the challenges and obstacles that lie before us in realizing the aims of this Treaty. But we move ahead with optimism and resolve. In the face of the catastrophic risks posed by nuclear weapons and in the interest of the very survival of humanity, we cannot do otherwise. We will take every path that is open to us, and work persistently to open those that are still closed. We will not rest until the last state has joined the Treaty, the last warhead has been dismantled and destroyed, and nuclear weapons have been totally eliminated from the Earth.

Draft Vienna Action Plan

1. This Action Plan was adopted by the States Parties at the First Meeting of States Parties of the Treaty on the Prohibition of Nuclear Weapons (TPNW) in Vienna, Austria, 21-23 June 2022.

2. The purpose of this Action Plan is to facilitate effective and timely implementation of the TPNW and its objectives and goals following the First Meeting of States Parties. The Plan sets out concrete steps and actions, and elaborates on roles and responsibilities. The actions are designed to guide States Parties and other relevant actors in the practical implementation of the Treaty, and thus to support States Parties in meeting their obligations, and furthering the Treaty's objective and purpose in a cooperative spirit among States Parties and other involved stakeholders.

3. Implementation and universalization of the TPNW are essential to achieving a world free of nuclear weapons and to addressing the harm caused by nuclear weapons to people and the environment.

4. With the following actions, the States Parties establish a framework to guide the implementation of the Treaty and set in motion processes to develop further areas of cooperation and implementation across the different provisions of the Treaty. The Vienna Action Plan details the actions States Parties will take during the intersessional period, primarily in preparation for the Second Meeting of States Parties but also beyond, in order to support implementation and universalization of the Treaty.

I. Universalization (Article 12)

5. Article 12 of the TPNW requires State Parties to "encourage States not party to the Treaty to sign, ratify, accept, approve or accede to the Treaty, with the goal of universal adherence of all States to the Treaty."

6. The situations and positions of states currently outside the Treaty differ widely. They include states already adhering to Nuclear-Weapon-Free Zones or having comparable national laws in place, States Parties to the Non-Proliferation Treaty (NPT) that do not possess nuclear weapons, and states currently relying on nuclear weapons for their security, including nuclear hosting states as well as nuclear-armed states. These differences need to be taken into account in implementing the universalization

obligation stipulated in Article 12. Therefore, universalization efforts are understood broadly, including through increasing signatures and ratifications, as well as promoting the underlying rationale of the total elimination of nuclear weapons due to their inherent risks and catastrophic humanitarian consequences. Universalization should serve as a strategy to maximize the authority of the Treaty`s core norms and principles in international politics. To this end,

States Parties resolve to:
   Action 1: Make universalization efforts a priority of States Parties. These efforts should focus on increasing the number of signatures and ratifications, as well as actively engaging in promoting the norms, values and underlying arguments of the Treaty, such as concern about the inherent risks and catastrophic humanitarian consequences of nuclear weapons, and the Treaty's effective contribution towards disarmament and international peace and security.
   Action 2: Call on all states that have not yet done so to sign and ratify the Treaty as soon as possible.
   Action 3: Promote universalization, including through ministerial or diplomatic *démarches* or outreach visits, either on their own or in a group of TPNW supporters, to capitals of non-state parties or at regional or other relevant organisations, highlighting the value of the Treaty and the political, legal and practical importance of signature and ratification.
   Action 4: Explore potential areas where further information to facilitate accession to the Treaty might be necessary, and potentially explore options to fill these gaps.
   Action 5: Share best practices and provide technical support for the ratification process, for example through capacity building activities, such as workshops and seminars, to explain the provisions of the TPNW in detail and help clarify the steps a prospective state party would have to undertake to implement the Treaty. To that end, parties will endeavour to utilise existing regional and multilateral frameworks, as feasible.
   Action 6: Appoint within 60 days national contact points for facilitating the implementation of Article 12.
   Action 7: Raise awareness of the Treaty at international conferences and regional workshops and seminars, as well as through the commissioning of studies and publications to promote the case for the TPNW.
   Action 8: Make every effort to increase the number of states voting in favour of the relevant resolutions before the UN General Assembly as a positive step in support of the Treaty.

Action 9: Highlight the importance of the TPNW in statements, including at the political level, through joint regional or cross-regional statements, and resolutions and in all relevant fora, including organs of the UN disarmament machinery.

Action 10: Highlight the humanitarian consequences of nuclear weapons, the risks associated with these weapons, and the legal and ethical questions regarding the use and the threat of use of nuclear weapons and the practice of nuclear deterrence.

Action 11: Cooperate with affected states not party to the Treaty to advance the objectives of the Treaty and to facilitate adherence to the Treaty.

Action 12: Engage with those States that for the moment remain committed to nuclear weapons and nuclear deterrence, *inter alia* by providing opportunities for dialogue, highlighting the underlying rationale of the Treaty and the humanitarian consequences of nuclear weapons and their inherent risks, and pursuing a fact-based approach in engaging with concerns or criticisms about the TPNW.

Action 13: Encourage and support involvement and active cooperation of all relevant partners and, to the extent possible, coordinate these universalization efforts to facilitate domestic ratification processes. These partners include the United Nations and the UN Secretary General, including UN regional centres for peace and disarmament, other international institutions and organizations, the International Committee of the Red Cross (ICRC), the International Campaign to Abolish Nuclear Weapons (ICAN) and other non-governmental organizations as well as parliamentarians and interested citizens.

Action 14: Share information on their universalization activities within the TPNW through reports to Meetings of States Parties or Review Conferences, updates to the informal contact group on universalization, or other appropriate means.

II. Towards the elimination of nuclear weapons (Article 4)

7. Article 4 of the TPNW is one of the fundamental precepts that establishes this legal instrument as a disarmament treaty and as part of the broader disarmament legal architecture. To achieve its disarmament goal, the TPNW envisages the designation of a competent international authority or authorities (IA(s)), with particular negotiation and verification mandates. This reflects the awareness of the TPNW´s negotiators that implementing Article 4 is a substantial endeavour that should be

undertaken in a considered and holistic manner.

8. There is no requirement for the designation of an IA(s) by the First Meeting of States Parties or by the entry into force of the Treaty for a State Party to which Article 4.1 or Article 4.2 applies. In this early stage of implementation of the Treaty, further reflection and work on developing such a mechanism with the input of State Parties, as well as relevant scientific and technical input is the most substantive and meaningful way to approach the implementation of these provisions. To this end,

States Parties resolve to:

> Action 15: Pursue further discussions during the intersessional period towards developing a coherent approach on matters related to a competent international authority or authorities (IA(s))-, from the general obligations of States Parties to the specific mandate of the IA(s), and providing guidance for the designation of IA(s).
>
> Action 16: Designate within 90 days national contact points with regard to the designation of the IA(s).
>
> Action 17: Elaborate during the intersessional period on the specific requirements of extension requests related to Article 4 of the Treaty for nuclear-armed states' destruction of nuclear weapons or other nuclear explosive devices in their ownership, possession or control (Article 4 (2)) and for the removal of such weapons or devices from nuclear hosting states (Article 4 (4)). This intersessional process should be based upon or informed by advice from the Scientific Advisory Group and information from relevant international technical agencies.
>
> Action 18: Commit their best efforts to advancing and supporting progress on nuclear disarmament verification, while recognizing that verification is not an end in itself, nor a substitute for nuclear disarmament, but a positive enabler for progress on disarmament.

III. Victim assistance, environmental remediation and international cooperation and assistance (Articles 6 and 7)

9. The TPNW's positive obligations are central to the humanitarian goals of the Treaty. They aim to address the harm from past use and testing of nuclear weapons as well as the ongoing and expected future harm from the resulting contamination. Articles 6 and 7 draw on similar provisions in other humanitarian disarmament treaties but they are the first of their kind in a nuclear weapons treaty. These articles are designed to address the human and environmental effects of nuclear weapons and to provide

affected States Parties with technical, material, and financial support to further the implementation of the Treaty. To this end,

States Parties resolve to:

Action 19: Engage with relevant stakeholders, including international organizations, civil society, affected communities, indigenous peoples, and youth, and work cooperatively to advance effective and sustainable implementation of Articles 6 and 7. In particular, they will closely consult with, actively involve, and disseminate information to, affected communities at all stages of the victim assistance and environmental remediation process.

Action 20: Engage and promote information exchange with states not party to the Treaty that have used or tested nuclear weapons, or any other nuclear explosive devices, on their provision of assistance to affected states parties for the purpose of victim assistance and environmental remediation.

Action 21: Establish national focal points for Articles 6 and 7, with appropriate contact details for consultations, no later than 3 months after the 1MSP.

Action 22: Adopt or adapt and implement relevant national laws and policies on Articles 6 and 7, where appropriate.

Action 23: Coordinate and develop mechanisms, where needed, to facilitate the provision, by States Parties in a position to do so, of the international cooperation and technical, material, and financial assistance that affected states parties may require to implement the Treaty's victim assistance and environmental remediation provisions. Mechanisms should match needs, which may arise at any stage of implementing Article 6, with offers of assistance.

Action 24: Cooperate with the UN system, relevant international, regional, or national organizations or institutions, relevant non-governmental organizations or institutions, the International Committee of the Red Cross, the International Federation of Red Cross and Red Crescent Societies, national Red Cross and Red Crescent Societies, and bilaterally, as appropriate, in the development of their implementation framework.

Action 25: Conduct all victim assistance, environmental remediation, and international cooperation and assistance activities in accordance, in particular, with the principles of accessibility, inclusivity, non-discrimination, and transparency and in coordination with affected communities, and provide victim assistance in a manner that is age- and gender-sensitive given the disproportionate impact of nuclear weapons use and testing on women and girls and indigenous people.

Action 26: Review the implementation framework as well as implementation of Articles 6 and 7 regularly, in particular as new information emerges and situations evolve, and draw, as appropriate, on lessons from implementation measures for positive obligations in other treaty regimes.

Action 27: Recognize the importance of information exchange for the implementation of Articles 6 and 7. To this end, consulting with, and bearing in mind the needs and constraints of, affected states, States Parties will develop guidelines for voluntary reporting on national measures related to victim assistance, environmental remediation, and international cooperation and assistance, including deadlines, as appropriate. In the development of these guidelines States Parties will draw on the input of relevant stakeholders, including international organizations, civil society, affected communities, indigenous peoples, and youth.

Action 28: Consider developing a voluntary and a non-burdensome format for reporting during the intersessional period before the 2MSP, in close cooperation with states concerned, taking into account best practices for reporting under other disarmament treaties. For affected States Parties, such reports could include the effects of nuclear weapons in their territory, their progress in implementing the Treaty's victim assistance and environmental remediation obligations, and where they may need external support. Other States Parties could report on what international cooperation and assistance they have provided, and on their outreach to states not party in support of their objectives of Articles 6 and 7.

Action 29: Discuss the feasibility of, and propose possible guidelines for, establishing an international trust fund for states that have been affected by the use or testing of nuclear weapons, taking into account relevant precedents for such a trust fund. The purpose of such a fund would be, inter alia, to provide aid to assist survivors and to support measures toward environmental remediation.

States Parties affected by nuclear weapons use or testing resolve to:

Action 30: Assess the effects of nuclear weapons use and testing with respect to areas under their jurisdiction or control, including, in particular, the needs of victims and contamination of the environment, as well as national capacities to address them. Initial assessments could focus on gathering existing knowledge about ongoing and expected effects, and current and planned responses to date, and determining what additional information is needed. These initial assessments should be completed by and shared with the 2MSP.

Action 31: Develop national plans for implementation of their victim assistance and environmental remediation obligations, which include budgets and timeframes. Such plans could be integrated into existing frameworks to increase efficiency, and international cooperation and assistance should be provided where needed to reduce the burden on affected States Parties. Affected States Parties should share their progress with the 2MSP.

States Parties in a position to do so resolve to:

Action 32: Act upon their obligation under Article 7 (3) to assist those States Parties with clearly demonstrated needs for external support, by contributing to the mobilization of resources and the provision of technical, material and financial assistance to States Parties affected by nuclear weapons use or testing, to further the implementation of this Treaty.

IV. Institutionalizing scientific and technical advice for the effective implementation of the TPNW

10. Further enriching the knowledge on the humanitarian impacts of nuclear weapons and a shared understanding of the risks of nuclear weapons as well as technical guidance for the implementation of Article 4 will be important to ensure the effective implementation of the Treaty. The establishment of the Scientific Advisory Group (SAG) aims to assist States Parties in implementing the Treaty and in strengthening the credibility of the implementation process. To this end,

States Parties resolve to:

Action 33: Support the work of the SAG, including through the appointment of recognized experts drawn from the broadest possible pool in the field of nuclear disarmament and non-proliferation, and/or the humanitarian consequences and risks associated with nuclear weapons, and the requisite humanitarian response, active at relevant institutions and universities on the basis of their expertise in the particular scientific fields relevant to the implementation of the TPNW.

Action 34: Identify and engage scientific and technical experts and institutions in TPNW States Parties by the 2MSP and, through the SAG, establish a geographically diverse and gender balanced network of experts to support the goals and TPNW.

V. The relationship of the TPNW with the nuclear disarmament and non-proliferation regime

11. While the TPNW is a stand-alone legally binding instrument, it builds upon, contributes to and complements a rich and diverse disarmament and non-proliferation architecture. In order to highlight and underscore these complementarities with specific disarmament instruments, particularly the NPT,

States Parties resolve to:
    Action 35: Emphasise the complementarity of the TPNW with the existing disarmament and non-proliferation regime at appropriate opportunities, including Preparatory Meetings and Review Conferences of the NPT, and with relevant multilateral nuclear disarmament-related initiatives and groupings.
    Action 36: Appoint an informal facilitator to further explore and articulate the possible areas of tangible cooperation between the TPNW and the NPT during the intersessional period, and provide support for the efforts of the informal facilitator.
    Action 37: Cooperate with other international bodies, such as the IAEA and the CTBTO, in order to enhance cooperation, including in the areas of nuclear safeguards and verification. Such cooperation should enhance the complementarity between the TPNW, the NPT and the CTBT.
    Action 38: Continue to work together on outreach projects in order to raise awareness, not only among governments, but also with civil society, academia, parliamentarians and the general public, including youth organizations, so as to highlight the complementarity between the TPNW and the existing disarmament and non-proliferation regime, including Nuclear-Weapon-Free Zone Treaties.

VI. Other matters essential for achieving the Treaty's aims

Principles of inclusivity and cooperation among stakeholders in the implementation of the Treaty

States Parties resolve to:

> Action 39: Meet their obligations in the Treaty's established spirit of cooperation, inclusivity and transparency, and to integrate gender considerations in across the work of the Treaty's implementation.
>
> Action 40: Cooperate closely with the United Nations, the International Committee of the Red Cross, the International Campaign to Abolish Nuclear Weapons, academia, affected communities and other civil society organisations.
>
> Action 41: Facilitate the active participation of relevant stakeholders, and take into account the different needs of people in affected communities and indigenous people and ensure strong ownership by all States Parties.
>
> Action 42: Contribute on a voluntary basis to initiatives to facilitate widespread representation at meetings of the Treaty.

Additional Aspects of Support for Treaty Implementation

12. The effective functioning and full implementation of the Treaty have been enhanced through the decisions taken at the First Meeting of States Parties to establish an intersessional structure that takes into account the requirements and resources available in this early phase of the TPNW.

States Parties resolve to:

> Action 43: Support the efforts of the Coordinating Committee and the informal working groups in their coordination of the intersessional work between MSPs.
>
> Action 44: Continue to reaffirm the valuable role of the United Nations in providing support to MSPs.
>
> Action 45: Enhance and make use of synergies between the Treaty and other relevant instruments of disarmament and of international humanitarian and human rights law to which TPNW States Parties are party.

Transparency and exchange of information

States Parties resolve to:

> Action 46: Fulfil their obligation to provide initial declarations under Article 2 without delay.

Implementing the Gender Provisions of the TPNW

13. As States Parties move forward with Treaty implementation, they should reflect on the gender-related provisions of the Treaty and consider specific implementation actions to operationalise them. To this end,

States Parties resolve to:

Action 47: Emphasize the gender-responsive nature of the TPNW and recommend that gender considerations are taken into account across all TPNW-related national policies, programs and projects.

Action 48: Establish a Gender Focal Point to work during the intersessional period to support the implementation of the gender provisions of the Treaty and report on progress made to the 2MSP.

Action 49: Begin work during the intersessional period to develop guidelines for ensuring age- and gender-sensitive Victim Assistance, taking into account relevant approaches in other humanitarian disarmament instruments.

Action 50: Begin work during the intersessional period to develop guidelines for the integration of gender perspectives in international cooperation and assistance, taking into account relevant approaches in other humanitarian disarmament instruments.

TPNW Dossier

The Spokesman 147 (*Challenging Nuclearism*) includes a 41 page dossier on the the Treaty on the Prohobition of Nuclear Weapons, including the text of the treaty and analysis from *Setsuko Thurlow* ('Through the doorway'), *Daryl G. Kimball* ('Turning Point'), *Beatrice Fihn & Daniel Högsta* ('Changing Europe's Calculations'), *Bertrand Russell* ('Disarmament') and *Richard Falk* ('Challenging Nuclearism').

£6 | 138 pages
ISBN 9780851248950
www.spokesmanbooks.org

Bruce Kent

22 June 1929 - 8 June 2022

Plain speaking

Bruce Kent

Bruce Kent's collected reviews for *The Spokesman* reveal not only an engaging intellect but also a very clear sense of purpose. The titles he reviewed and his rigorous interrogation of the ideas presented within them show an enduring commitment to peace. Even where he found much to agree with, Bruce always had an insight not otherwise addressed in the text.

As Bruce reflects in his autobiography, *Undiscovered Ends* (Harper Collins, 1992):

'In one lifetime I have already had more than my share of privileges. Above all I have been blessed with a sense of purpose which still hasn't faded. In the field I know best there is still much to do in a world which can spend even now nearly a trillion dollars a year on war and the preparations for it. One day it is going to dawn on the human race that war is as barbaric a means of resolving conflict as cannibalism is a means of coping with dietary deficiency. If we had only read the right parts of the right books we might have learned long ago:

> A King is not saved by his great army,
> A warrior is not delivered by his great strength.
> The war horse is a vain hope for victory and by its great strength it cannot save.
> *Psalm 33*

"One day" can be a long way off. However, it seems to me that we are now in the middle of a Copernican revolution in understanding, which some have not yet begun to notice ...'

* * *

Bertrand Russell

Bertrand Russell, *Common Sense and Nuclear Warfare*, Routledge, 2001, 112pp, £45.00 hardback, ISBN 0 41524 994 5, £8.99 paperback, ISBN 0 41524 995 3

Thanks to the Bertrand Russell Peace Foundation we now have this new edition of a book which first appeared in 1959. I was not one who read it the first time round, and therefore it was interesting indeed to see how lasting and contemporary the Russell warnings of 1959 still are.

Yet so much has changed. Nuclear weapons have spread to at least eight countries. Largely unnoticed, two countries – Ukraine and South Africa – have actually possessed nuclear weapons but have independently relinquished them. We have been through the lunacies of the Cold War, with nuclear weapons reaching levels which even George Kennan, one-time United States hawk, described as grotesque. We have, by the grace of God or sheer good luck, survived a whole series of accidents and misperceptions which could easily have resulted in catastrophic nuclear exchange.

Thanks to the lobbying and expertise of those involved in the World Court Project, we now have the 1996 advisory opinion of the International Court of Justice. That opinion makes it clear that in current circumstances the threat and use of nuclear weapons would actually be illegal. However, that was not a unanimous opinion of the judges. What was unanimous was their ruling that the nuclear powers have a legal obligation to start and complete negotiations aimed at the elimination of all their nuclear weapons. There are still no such negotiations in progress.

Is Russell's book relevant to all this nearly 50 years later? Very much so. There is much that is very contemporary. The Greens of today would certainly take him to their hearts: '…when I read of plans to defile the heavens by the petty squabbles of the animated lumps that disgrace a certain planet, I cannot but feel that the men who make these plans are guilty of a kind of impiety.' Theologians of a peaceful bent would warm to that word impiety as we contemplate the possibility of circling satellites armed with pinpoint lasers targeting the earth every minute of the day. Scientists and politicians get a practical reminder. 'The spread of power without wisdom is utterly terrifying'. Russell even looks forward to a demilitarised world in which there could be for everyone 'a life of joy such as the past has never known'.

His reputation is that of a rather eccentric prophet of doom urging instant action to avert immediate disaster. This book shows him to have been not only idealistic but highly practical. Clear steps are proposed for United Nations reform. Stages on the way to general disarmament are laid out in pragmatic fashion. Though he clearly believed in unilateral nuclear disarmament for Britain, he makes no such proposals for the major powers. Perhaps some proposals are so far into the future as to seem bizarre even today. What would the Royal Navy think of crewing its submarines with sailors 'of different nations so that mutiny in some national interest would be impossible'? That sounds odd, but is it really so different from the UN peacekeeping forces of today, drawn from many different countries but deployed together in a common cause?

The dangers of aggressive nationalism which Russell describes have not gone away. There is happily today strong public support for the development of democratic globalism as opposed to selfish corporate globalism. Russell's stress on education is quite inspiring. 'It should be one of the tasks of education to make vivid in the minds of the young both the merits of the civilised way of life and the needless dangers to which it is exposed…'

The book comes with a very contemporary 27-page foreword by Ken Coates, who knew Russell well, and it starts out with a commendation from Noam Chomsky. One critical note. I did not find very satisfactory, or even convincing, Russell's attempt to justify his suggested threats in the late 1940s of military action against the pre-nuclear Soviet Union. But then some great men with more than average egos find it hard to admit inconsistencies or mistakes. The same goes for lesser men, too.

Russell's little book is well worth reading even now, long after it first appeared. Plenty of people are always wrapped up in the problems of the day. Too few can look to the long future with hope. Russell clearly did.

The Spokesman 74, 2002

Human Action

Conor Foley, *The Thin Blue Line: How Humanitarianism Went to War*, Verso, 256 pages, hardback ISBN 9781844672899, £ 14.99

This provocative, informative and useful book is well worth reading. Essential reading in fact for anyone who is serious about building a more just international order, and who is ready to start from where we are, not from where we would like to be.

The author seems to have landed up in nearly every crisis location – Uganda, Kosovo, Angola, Bosnia, Colombia, Sri Lanka and Indonesia –

under one or another humanitarian umbrella in recent years. His theme is the relationship between humanitarian activity, which ought to make human need, rather than borders, its priority, and the State sovereignty on which the United Nations (and most of the political world, since Westphalia) has been based.

My own belief is that the UN never did confer on states quite the sovereignty that they now claim for themselves. Article 2.7 of the UN Charter affirms that the charter does nothing 'to authorise the UN to intervene in matters which are essentially within the domestic jurisdiction of any state'. Surely, there is an open door for the lawyers. What is domestic jurisdiction? Can a state claim that such jurisdiction overrides the obligations set out in the 1948 Declaration of Human Rights? It does not, of course, follow that, as the book rather implies, military intervention is the only or the most effective form of intervention. In Kosovo, the observers of the Organisation for Security and Co-operation in Europe (OSCE) did a very effective job, until they were thrown out by those who had sent them there, and the NATO militarists took over.

Intervention of any kind is now suspect because it has been used too often for national priorities other than humanitarian, and very selectively. We will live with the lies of Iraq for a very long time. No one is suggesting, for obvious practical reasons, military intervention on behalf of the beleaguered and blockaded inhabitants of Gaza, for instance. Nor it is it being suggested on behalf of the occupied inhabitants of Tibet.

There are questions still to be answered. Why did we do our best to maintain the unity of Federal Nigeria when Biafran secession was the issue, but do our best to break up the Yugoslav federation when Croatian and Slovenian secession was the issue?

Who are all these humanitarian non-governmental organisations referred to frequently in the book? Is the Campaign Against the Arms Trade one of them? If not, why not? I suspect that it is the Oxfams and the Christian Aids who qualify, not the groups with more radical programmes.

The author fairly recognises many of the problems. Of NGO work in general he concludes that, while such activity can 'prick the world's conscience that "something must be done" simultaneously it reinforces the delusion that humanitarian action can ever be enough'.

I would have liked more stress on the obvious truth, which is that the real work of the agencies is to awaken their home populations to the need for radical political action and cultural change. After all, the budgets of all the agencies put together are miniscule by comparison with national budgets, and worse than miniscule when looked at alongside the trillion and quarter dollars the world spends on weapons and war every year. The unjust way in which we run our world is a permanent ongoing disaster in its own right.

The author recognises that some agencies are committed to playing safe. How well I remember little Operation Omega, based in Calcutta in 1971, bravely running through East Pakistan's borders and refusing to use any name but that of Bangladesh. Quite unlike Save the Children, who stuck to 'East Pakistan' until the Foreign Office declared that it was safe to do otherwise. It was in Calcutta, too, that I saw first-hand the competitive nature of NGO work. Who got what time on television and radio, so that activity was noted, and donors encouraged at home, was a major part of NGO concern. The bottom line is always there even in the world of altruism.

I hope this book will push many to ask questions and to take action. We need an International Criminal Court which has the teeth to deal with the major violators of international law, not just the nastier small fish. We need a range of non-military as well as military/ policing options in advance for when the time comes for legitimate UN-authorised intervention to protect the innocent from cruelty and violence.

Most of all, we need a people with a sense of involvement in the reality of political power. We, in the nice liberal democratic West, deceive ourselves if we think we have influence in international affairs. Most people have never seen the UN Charter or the Declaration of Human Rights. Few could name those who represent our country on the various important UN agencies. Vital reports like that of the 1978 Special Session on Disarmament gather dust on shelves.

The great merit of *The Thin Blue Line* is that it will stir some into activity. It is not only Obama who thinks that the future is ours to make.

The Spokesman 103, 2009

Conscience

Ozgur Heval Cinar and Coskun Usterci, *Conscientious Objection: Resisting Militarised Society*, Zed Books, 272 pages, hardback ISBN 9781848132771, £75, paperback ISBN 9781848132788, £19.99

This interesting and, at times, mildly irritating book is a very useful contribution to the scholarship of conscientious objection. It consists of twenty-three essays, the majority of which have been written by Turkish authors. Many were presented at a conference on this subject held in January 2007 at Istanbul's Bilgi University. Granted the cultural and legal hostility to conscientious objection in Turkey, it is a surprise that the conference went ahead at all. But then the Turkish Government wants to prove its European credentials. Already a member of the Council of Europe, it wants to be granted membership of the European Union as well. In this area of human rights it has a long way to go to catch up with the rest of Europe. Essay after essay makes this very clear indeed.

There are ways of escaping Turkish conscription, but they are not based on any legal recognition of human rights. Homosexuality is one ground for exemption, but the ways in which sexual orientation has to be proved are disgusting beyond belief.

The book is not only concerned with the situation in Turkey. There are contributions covering Greece, Spain, Chile, South Africa and other countries. The description of what went on, in the past, in Spain rang a few bells with me. I well remember being told, by an official at the Spanish Embassy in London, that 'to be a Spaniard and a catholic is to be a soldier'. This was their response to our Pax Christi opposition to the cat and mouse game played by the Franco Government with the lives of young men refusing to fight in the colonial African wars. As in many other countries, it was the Jehovah's Witnesses who led the way and who suffered greatly in regimes on both sides of the communist/capitalist divide.

An interesting book, but why is it irritating? Because there seems to be an underlying conviction expressed by many that objectors who are not inspired by a collective desire to reform society, but who base their decisions on personal and moral grounds, are somehow second class citizens in the world of conscientious objection. The real CO needs to be 'anti-patriarchal, anti-heteronormative, anti-homophobic and pro-feminist', one author suggests. Some of my heroes amongst those who have refused at great cost, such as Franz Jagerstatter who was executed in August '43, had no notion of social change at all. But they stood and died for a moral principle.

It is also a little irritating that the reader is meant to have more than working knowledge of European legal and political structures. Without such knowledge it is difficult to follow the ramifications of the legal road to the recognition of conscientious objection as a human right.

The 'historical' essays were of great interest to me. I had no idea how much influence Prussian militarism had on the Turkish state long before Attaturk arrived on the scene. Universal conscription we owe of course to Napoleon, but it was refined and polished by Kaiser Wilhelm 1, who launched the phrase about 'the nation in arms'.

The Prussians set about the wholesale militarisation of the state. Said a German-trained Turkish Staff major, in 1908, 'there is no separation between the army and the nation'.

'Peace time should be regarded as the continuation of wartime without fighting,' said another. Militarised as our own British society is today, we have little idea of how the army still dominates in Turkish life, which is why granting rights to conscientious objectors is so difficult.

The global statistics are of great interest too. There are at the moment 192 'sovereign' states. More than 20 have no armed forces. 168 of them do and 80 of those rely on volunteer forces. Some 88 still depend on conscription. Turkey is the only member of the Council of Europe not to grant alternative service rights to COs. There are devious ways of escaping service in Turkey, so it is probably only the most honest and straightforward who find themselves in head-on collision with the law.

What the book does not deal with is how we can resist the claims of a militarised society even if we are not confronted with the call to arms. Supporting 'Conscience', once known as the Peace Tax Campaign, is one such way. Choice of occupation is another. I have always felt that when Joseph Rotblat refused to continue to work on the atomic bomb, in 1944, that his was a CO stance.

Not everything can go into 272 pages. There is more than enough in this book to make it both important and useful.

The Spokesman 106, 2009

Diego Garcia

David Vine, *Island of Shame: The secret history of the US military base on Diego Garcia*, Princeton University Press, 282 pages, hardback ISBN 9780691138695, £20.95

I got angrier and angrier as I read this book. It is a story of ruthless military and economic imperialism, Cold War driven, and underpinned by servile British governments. Diego Garcia is today only one of a thousand military bases which the United States has in other countries. No wonder the Russians and the Chinese see themselves as encircled.

Diego Garcia is a large island military base which dominates the South Asia region, and played a major part in both the Iraq wars. It first came to the attention of US military planners because they were looking for locations for air and naval bases which would not be subject to opposition later on from hostile populations or nationalistic governments. Unoccupied islands were ideal for that purpose.

So Diego Garcia came into focus. There were, however, two problems. It was part of Mauritius, a British colony, and it certainly was populated, if by only a few thousand inhabitants – but they had been there at least for two centuries.

The colonial problem was solved, on behalf of the Americans, by the British, who made a major financial grant to the future leaders of Mauritius with the promise that independence would be speeded up. The price tag was that the islands, of which Diego Garcia was one, would be cut off from Mauritius. This involved ignoring the spirit, if not the letter, of article 73 of the UN Charter, which said that, in the transition period from colonialism to independence, 'the interests of the inhabitants … are paramount'. The division was effected, and a new administrative structure was set up in 1965: the British Indian Ocean Territory.

At least one British Secretary of State for the Colonies, Francis Pakenham (the author does not know that he is naming our Lord Longford) was quite honest. He suggested that we should just tell the UN that, in this case, we did not intend to accept that Article 73 was binding. Other civil servants and government officials were more devious. Said one: 'The legal position of the inhabitants would be greatly simplified from our point of view – though not necessarily from theirs – if we decided to treat them as a floating population'.

Another, Alan Brook Taylor, suggested turning them into residents of Mauritius. 'This device, though rather transparent, would at least give us a defensible position.' Worse comments came from Sir Paul Gore-Booth and D.A. Greenhill (later Baron), whose racist and sexist comments have to be seen to be believed. The aim was clear: empty the islands and prepare for US occupation.

That is exactly what happened. The first some Chagossians knew about it was when they were told, when trying to return from a hospital visit to Mauritius, that there was to be no return. So it went on, until in 1971 an entire ship-full were dispatched, in disgraceful conditions, away from their homes for good. In a disgusting piece of brutality, their pet dogs were gassed in a shed as the inhabitants were leaving. An empty island means just that.

The future of those expelled has been hard. They have been given minor compensation grants but, for the most part, they have lived in poverty. Unemployment has been the norm. Their efforts to get the legal right to return at one stage looked hopeful, but this was eventually blocked by the House of Lords.

Meanwhile, the base now employs other imported workers, and the harbour has become a yacht haven for tourists as well as a military location.

There are strong indications also that the island has been used for 'rendition' flights.

Ironically, the American who promoted the whole idea of safe US island bases had a change of heart at the end of his days. Too late, Stuart Barber came to understand how his schemes had ruined the lives of innocent people far away, and wanted justice to be done. His pleas were not heeded, and his letters ignored.

There is one gap in the story. What were international human rights nongovernmental organisations doing at the time, both in the United Kingdom and on Mauritius, to protect these victims? Bishop Trevor Huddleston, whose name does not appear in this book, was actually Bishop of Mauritius for some years immediately after the expulsion. Did he, with his anti-apartheid record, not speak out? We are not told.

This moving and very informative book is not well served by its maps. They are quite inadequate. If there is to be a second edition, as I hope and recommend, then let there be more detailed maps of the Indian Ocean area. For instance, where are the Seychelles, another set of islands which might also have been turned into a base?

The Spokesman 107, 2010

Keep Talking

Mark Perry, *How to Lose the War on Terror*, Hurst Publishers 2010, 270 pages, hardback ISBN 9781850659624, £37.45, paperback ISBN 9781850659631, £12.99

This is a book which gets more and more interesting as the pages turn. It started life as a series of articles in the Asian Times in 2005. Then it developed into a book project when the author became involved, in 2005 and 2006, in attempts to dialogue with the Sunni resistance in northern Iraq. It became a full-blown book after further involvement with Hamas and Hezbollah leaders in Palestine and Lebanon.

The message which runs through it all is clear: 'Jaw Jaw is better than War War'. Perhaps, granted the hints now emerging from Afghanistan of talks with the Taliban, we are beginning, at last, to learn that lesson there. We ought to have learnt it decades ago during the Northern Ireland civil war.

The book starts with a very good quotation from that remarkable historian Barbara Tuchman:

'To halt the momentum of an accepted idea, to re-examine assumptions, is a disturbing process and requires more courage than Governments can usually summon'.

The entrenched idea in this case is that military power can defeat armed resistance which has some level of popular support. It can't. Sooner or later there have to be talks with 'the enemy'. There are always differing political aims, which have to be faced. Slapping labels on insurgents and calling them terrorists only manufactures yet more real terrorists.

The author's experience in Northern Iraq several years after the 2003 invasion is fascinating. It was, in fact, the United States military and the Civil Affairs group who responded to an invitation from some influential Iraqi exiles in Amman. Their up-front aim was to help to rebuild the Iraqi economy, but discussions went much further than that. So far, in fact, that hostile but significant people such as Paul Wolfowitz slammed down the shutters with a vengeance and humiliated the officials involved. His understanding of the situation, and I am sure others shared his ideas, was simple: 'Don't you know that these people are all Nazis?'

The official United States line was that there could be no talks with those they defined as terrorists. That is not even true according to their own past practice. The PLO and ANC and the opposition in Iraq were all called terrorists in their time, but US discussions went on with them nevertheless.

The chapters on Hamas, Hezbollah and Israel all tell the same story. There is an interesting quotation from a senior Hamas leader about the explicit clause in their Charter calling for the destruction of Israel, which is hardly compatible, anyway, with the Hamas offer of a ten-year truce. Says he: 'The Charter is not the Koran - it can be amended'.

There might have been a very different story to tell about the Middle East if the United States had not mounted such heavy opposition to the democratic result of the 2006 Palestinian elections. All CIA stops, at the orders of President Bush, were pulled out to make a Fatah/Hamas partnership impossible. Hamas leaders wanted to talk but their terrorist label made that impossible. Condoleezza Rice's staff were clear. The Secretary of State 'doesn't talk to terrorists'.

Probably all readers of this book will begin to wonder if we are not following much the same path as that of the United States. Islamaphobia is now spreading in Britain. Many Muslims see themselves as a people under threat. Expulsions and imprisonment, or the indefinite house prison of control orders, without knowledge of accuser or accusations, are now normal. Yet this is in the land of Habeas Corpus. If Bin Laden is still alive he must be delighted. There is no better way to provide him with more local recruits. Those responsible, at Government level, for our security would do well to read Mark Perry's interesting book.

The Spokesman 111, 2011

Afghanistan

Bob Woodward, *Obama's Wars – The Inside Story*, Simon & Schuster 2010, 464 pages, ISBN 9780857200440, £20

Even though this book is really only about one war – Afghanistan – it is a very revealing story. More than that, it is also an astonishing one for reasons that the author would not have had in mind. The dysfunctional relationship between the White House and the Pentagon, which this book reveals, is quite scary. These are the same people who make nuclear weapon decisions.

The book is a blow-by-blow, meeting-by-meeting account of the way in which, during 2009, a policy was agreed which resulted in Obama's statement about Afghanistan of November 2009. He announced then, after all these discussions, that there would be a troop increase (not as large as the Pentagon wanted) and, most significantly, the start of a military withdrawal in July 2011.

There are several surprises. Since Afghanistan is meant to be a UN/NATO operation, no one seems to have thought of consulting their so-called partners in the run-up to this decision. Ban Ki-Moon does not even appear in the index. British forces get the briefest mention. Even so, they get more than is given to those of the other countries with troops deployed.

Solutions to problems are overwhelmingly framed in military terms. 'The man who is equipped only with a hammer sees every problem as a nail' rings true on every page. Obama, with Vietnam in mind, is clearly desperate to get out of the Afghanistan swamp. He is, however, squeezed at every point by the military. His Vice-President, Joe Biden, has, perhaps, the most original ideas, but he gets marginalized.

There is no evidence that any one realises that the United States is not thought, by the rest of the world, to be God's gift to world order. No one asks why terrorists take to terrorism or if insurgents have some reason for insurging – if I may invent a word. At one point, even an intelligent man like the President himself says 'We don't seek world domination or occupation'. The 1,000 US bases and military facilities strung around the world tell a different story to most of us.

US connivance in the occupation of Palestine or the slaughter in Iraq, as reasons for Muslim hostility, gets no mention. Palestine itself is not even in the index. It is indeed revealing that Pakistan, with its eyes on India, has played such an ambivalent role in the whole conflict.

In a rather *Readers' Digest* style the author describes in detail all the various lengthy top level meetings that went on before the November announcement. I had to wonder how Obama sleeps at night, and when he has time to think about the other pressing problems on his mind.

Thankfully, the book starts with a helpful list of all the participants, military, diplomatic and White House. The reader is left with no idea where the lines of authority actually run. Loyalty to the President, much trumpeted, is actually in short supply. Time and again the military come back to challenge his views with amendments, alternative suggestions and even media contradictions. This habit is not just a military weakness. Robert Gates, Secretary of Defence, tells a dinner gathering in Washington, at which President Karzai is present, 'we are not leaving Afghanistan prematurely … in fact we are not leaving at all'. This was exactly the opposite of the Obama position, which all had agreed to support. General Petraeus, the new commander in Afghanistan, says more privately, 'this is the kind of fight we're in for the rest of our lives and probably our kids' lives'.

This is a very important book which ought to be studied carefully. It is not the details of the discussions that matter or the pecking order of infights amongst the military, of which there are plenty. What it reveals is how the most powerful country in the world in military terms actually makes up its mind on critical international issues. The United Nations is a distant sideshow, as are the rest of us. NATO, an arm of US policy, is simply a means of disguising the reality.

The book has, too, a sad taste of tragedy. A decent man, suddenly given great world power, who knows where he wants to go, is impeded, but not yet brought to a halt, by forces, military and political, which are more powerful than he is.

The Spokesman 111, 2011

Not Using the Bomb

T.V. Paul, *The Tradition of Non-use of Nuclear Weapons*, Stanford University Press, 336 pages, paperback ISBN 9780804761321, £26.95

This book will be of great historical interest to anyone who needs a handy reminder about the various nuclear weapon crises which have threatened the world since 1945. It is primarily written for the academic defence world, so will not be at all points entirely intelligible to those outside that world. What is 'an eclectic framework which gives importance to rational and normative considerations' etc, etc? Nevertheless, there are an excellent series of page notes, an extensive index and a lengthy bibliography.

The book is exactly about what its title says. The author suggests that an international norm has developed since 1945 about the non-use of nuclear weapons, even in extreme circumstances. He does not, of course, deny that by their very deployment they are anything other than an ongoing threat. That is what they are for. Nevertheless, despite crisis after crisis, they have not been exploded during hostilities, despite their massive cost, since the fateful days of August 1945.

Why, since then, have all the nuclear weapon states refrained from using nuclear weapons? This question needs an answer. The most militarised country in the world, the United States of America, submitted itself to the most humiliating defeat possible in Vietnam with its last minute rush from Saigon. Not quite as humiliating, perhaps, but the Soviets can hardly have been proud of their withdrawal from Afghanistan. Why did the United States allow their allies, the French, to be defeated by their one time colonial subjects in Vietnam? Was Mrs Thatcher really ready to use nuclear weapons in the case of a looming conventional defeat in the Falklands?

Tracking the history of all this cannot have been easy. What exactly American Presidents said they would do, and what they did do, were often different things. What was said for sabre-rattling purposes and what was an actual intention? Perhaps the world has been fortunate in the leaders it has had. There were certainly those in the Oval Office during the Cuba crisis who, had they been in charge, would have uncorked the nuclear bottle.

If non-use is now a norm, that is not the greatest comfort. We have experienced too many nuclear weapon accidents in the last decades for comfort. I still think we owe our survival to the brave common sense of a Soviet Officer, Colonel Petrov, who, in 1983, refused to report what he thought he had seen – an incoming flight of nuclear-armed missiles from the West.

Why has a non-use norm developed, if indeed it has? The answers are complex but they have plenty to do with reputation, personal liability and law. It took until 1996 before the International Court of Justice gave its somewhat elastic ruling on the illegality of the use of nuclear weapons. If using nuclear weapons involved committing wars crimes, then someone in a leadership role might have realised that international disgrace and even criminal charges might be the consequence. Certainly, the longer the time elapsed since August 1945, and the nuclear bombing of Japan, the more difficult it would have been to use such barbaric weapons once more.

Yet, despite growing commitment to non-use, the Western side of the Cold War built a whole nuclear strategy on the possibility of winning wars actually fought with nuclear weapons. 'First use' was a deeply entrenched strategy, underpinned with weapons labelled 'tactical' that were designed for first use.

In 1984, General Chalupa, Commander in Chief in Europe, said 'Nato's strategy of first use is founded on the principles of flexible response – threatening an aggressor with direct defence and deliberate escalation to include the first use of nuclear weapons'.

I hope T.V. Paul is right and that we have permanently moved to a world of nuclear non-use. I do not, however, hold my breath. The major nuclear powers continue to frustrate progress towards a nuclear-weapon-abolition Convention. The consequence will be that nuclear weapons will, sooner or later, fall into the hands of state or non-state actors who may not be panicked by threats of mass destruction or fear of suicide. Accidents will continue to happen. Abolition is the only genuine security available.

The Spokesman 112, 2011

Hammered

Shannon D. Beebe and Mary Kaldor, *The Ultimate Weapon Is No Weapon: Human Security and the New Rules of War and Peace*, Public Affairs, 2010, 288 pages, ISBN 9781586488239 £15.99

When I first saw *The Ultimate Weapon Is No Weapon* – the title of this book – my heart lifted. It's going, I thought, to be about the uselessness of nuclear weapons and the ongoing insecurity which they ensure. I was wrong. The 'ultimate weapon' of the title is war itself. The message, coming from two very different authors, is the same. We cannot today, if ever we could, achieve security just by military means. Yet we annually spend globally some $1,630,000,000,000 attempting to do so. By far the largest slice of this enormous expenditure is the responsibility of the United States alone.

Real human security today means freedom from 'poverty, disease, violence and tyranny'. To achieve such goals, in the view of the authors, there has to be some kind of partnership between the civilian and the military world. In making her case Mary Kaldor, in particular, has shown great courage in visiting war zones in many places, some certainly very dangerous. How well I remember the kidnapping of Norman Kember [in Iraq] and the long wait and many vigils before he was released.

Mary is, of course, an academic, and Director of the Centre for the Study of Global Governance at the London School of Economics. She played an influential part in the Helsinki process and the European Nuclear Disarmament campaign in the 1980s.

Shannon Beebe is a United States Lieutenant Colonel who was attached to the US Embassy in Angola when the book was written. He played a major role in the establishment of the US Unified Command for Africa (AFRICOM) – which I don't like the sound of at all. It exists apparently 'to support US Government objectives'.

I am not sure that their new redefinition of security as human security is quite as new as they suggest. Some have travelled before on that road. Pope Paul VI in his letter Populorum Progressio of 1967 deserves a bit of credit. The 4th Section of that document is even headed 'Development is the new name for Peace'.

No matter. The lesson has still to be learnt by politicians and military alike. Influential people still behave as if they can bomb people into peace. 'The man who is equipped only with a hammer sees every problem as a nail' still describes the illusions under which most of the military suffer.

What is new about this book is the recommendation that there ought to be some sort of partnership between the military and the many nongovernmental organisations who flock to war zones bringing with them zeal and compassion certainly, but often also competition for publicity and funds.

The authors both agree that there is a 'role for force in human security operations' – but this is not quite the same as waging war for peace. Far more important is to try to make sure that any military action is aimed at the establishment of human rights and the basic standards of human life – food, education, medical provision and political rights – which we take for granted. Indeed, military action is only legitimate, according to Article 42 of the UN Charter, when the Security Council is satisfied that all peaceful means of resolving conflict have been exhausted.

Condoleezza Rice has yet to learn such lessons. In a interview for the New York Times in 2000, quoted in this book, she said of such a new approach 'Carrying out civil administration and police functions is simply going to degrade the American capability to do the things America has to do. We don't need to have the 82 Airborne escorting kids to kindergarten'. Perhaps America does not have to do the things that some Americans think they have to do.

This is a stimulating and even optimistic book, which humanitarian NGOs as well as the military ought to read. Its focus is clearly on the recent overseas wars in which, unhappily, we have been involved. If we are moving away from a world of war to one of global policing and community building, so much the better.

I would have liked, however, to have heard more about the current global culture of war which so dominates today in education and the media. We cannot export a culture of peace and a respect for human rights unless they also flourish in the world of wealth and power.

The Spokesman 115, 2012

The Art of Peace

John Gittings, *The Glorious Art of Peace: From the Iliad to Iraq*, Oxford University Press 2012, 316 pages illustrated, hardback ISBN 9780199575763, £18.99

This is an impressive book of scholarship and personal conviction. It comes with a substantial list of notes and a useful general index. All who are working for world peace will find it a great source of information and encouragement. The final sentence, a quotation from Nobel Prize winner Linus Pauling, about our 'unique epoch' sums it all up:

> 'We are privileged to have the opportunity of contributing to the achievement of the goal of the abolition of war and its replacement by world law.'

Gittings takes us from ancient Greek history right up to Afghanistan and Iraq. Ignorance prevents me from commenting on Chinese and Greek peace and war history, about which Gittings clearly knows a great deal. Such history evidently was not always bloody and violent. There is a picture of quaint Chinese stone carvings of domestic calm to prove it. More at home with Shakespeare's dramas, I regret that in so much school literature we concentrated on single set books rather than on the range of an author's work. Gittings seems to know all Shakespeare's plays by heart. There is, as he makes clear, so much more to Shakespeare than Laurence Olivier in Henry V telling his countrymen that they would regret missing out on the chance to bump off Frenchmen.

Other names which have a place in the tradition of peacemaking will be familiar to many readers: Augustine, Erasmus, More, Kant, de Sellon, Czar Nicholas II, Bertha von Suttner and Jane Adams. At home in Britain we have Cobden, Henry Richard, Lord Cecil of League of Nations Union fame, Vera Brittain and Joseph Rotblat. These are only a few of those who have worked over the centuries, in various parts of the world, towards a time when differences will be settled by law and arbitration and not by war and violence.

There has been much progress, as Gittings makes clear , but some sad near misses as well. I did not know how close we came, with the Hoover Plan, to having a successful League of Nations Disarmament Conference, in 1932, or how largely Britain was responsible for its failure. No wonder Sylvia Pankhurst put up her ironic 'Bomb' statue outside her house in Epping.

Some of the numbers and achievements in terms of grassroots organising are, by today's standards, astonishing. The League of Nations Union had, in its heyday, some 400,000 members, and was able to organise, in 1934, with the help of other organisations, a national ballot in support of the League which collected personal replies from over 10 million citizens. Far from being a pacifist ballot, well over half of those responding wanted the League to be able to take military action against aggressors.

The United Nations followed the League. Its Charter was signed in June 1945, before the end of World War Two. Its first aim was 'to save succeeding generations from the scourge of war'. In that task it has arguably failed, though in many others it has succeeded beyond expectation. Like the late, and equally UN minded, Erskine Childers, Gittings is sure that in so many areas – education, human rights, health and even the environment – much has been achieved. That more could have been done is only too true, but, granted the road blocks set up by the great powers in the Security Council, the General Assembly has perhaps too often felt itself to be incapable, or scared, of independent action.

Gittings is clear that, despite the failures, we have made substantial progress towards a world of peaceful citizenship under the rule of law. The obstacles in front of us are obvious. A conformist media willing to repeat any claim coming from political power, an arms industry which needs threats and fears to make its money, and a crude nationalism which prevents real internationalist thought.

As malign as ever is the 1947 nationalistic demand from Ernest Bevin, which took Britain down the nuclear weapon road. He had to have, he said, a nuclear weapon 'with a bloody great Union Jack on top'. Such crudity, then and now, makes for slow progress in what Gittings calls the Art of Peace.

The Spokesman 120, 2013

* * *

Bruce Kent
1929-2022

Like many others, I benefited from Bruce Kent's long ministry to the peace movement. On 18 May 2022, we celebrated Bertrand Russell's 150th birthday at Conway Hall in London. Bruce came and sat in the front row. The next day, he wrote to say 'Well done yesterday --- that was a warm, friendly and informative afternoon'. Bruce was spontaneously humorous and encouraging, and he is greatly missed.

Bruce became general secretary of CND in 1980, about the same time I started as a volunteer with the Bertrand Russell Peace Foundation in Nottingham. Ken Coates of the Foundation was teaching an adult education course about power and politics in Britain, which I joined. Labour had lost the 1979 general election and, in 1980, Mrs Thatcher was soon to join President elect Ronald Reagan in escalating the nuclear arms race with the Soviet Union, following the USSR's ill-judged invasion of Afghanistan in December 1979. US nuclear-armed cruise missiles were to be located at two redundant US airbases in England and in five other NATO member states, as well as super-fast Pershing missiles in what was then West Germany. The Soviet Union was already deploying its own mobile short and medium range nuclear weapons. The talk was of 'limited' nuclear war in Europe, the likely 'theatre' of devastating conflict.

In his autobiography, *Undiscovered ENDs*, Bruce recounts how 'providence' seemed to steer him towards stewardship of CND at that time. Such benevolent providence would be most welcome. Bruce exuded warmth and humanity as a priestly figurehead of the rainbow cavalcade which was the international peace movement bestirring in the early 1980s. The Russell Foundation was busy circulating the Appeal for European

Nuclear Disarmament '… to free the entire territory of Europe, from Poland to Portugal, from nuclear weapons, air and submarine bases, and from all institutions engaged in research into or manufacture of nuclear weapons'. The Appeal had been drafted by Edward Thompson, Ken Coates, Mary Kaldor and others, developing an idea originated by Ralph Miliband. The Appeal was launched in April 1980. There was an enthusiastic response. Signatories from many European countries endorsed the call for a representative conference of all those signing the END or 'Russell Appeal', as it was known in some places. In due course, the END Conventions began their annual gatherings, commencing in Brussels in 1982.

Organisationally in Britain, END's first years were not without problems. An inaugural meeting took place at Friends House, Euston Road, on a Saturday afternoon in the early summer of 1980. Bruce was probably there. Mike Cooley and Arthur Scargill certainly were, alongside Ken Coates, Ken Fleet, Mary Kaldor and Claude Bourdet, the French writer who had fought with the Resistance. He had travelled from Paris. Dorothy and Edward Thompson were probably there. That meeting went well. The differences arose later within the END co-ordinating committee in Britain. Bruce regularly participated in meetings of the co-ordinating committee. I recall attending one meeting at the House of Commons where Stuart Holland MP hosted us. He took us past Westminster Hall where Bruce was moved to remark 'Thomas More — right there!', referring to the saint's trial for treason in 1535. Stuart took us to lunch in a small canteen where Bruce demolished steaming jam roly-poly, while Peter Shore MP gawped at Edward Thompson. Peggy Duff, CND's first and highly adventurous General Secretary, lent some fizz and experience to proceedings. Sadly, she died in April 1981. Later, the END co-ordinating committee tended to meet at the office in Endsleigh Street, where Meg Beresford, Ben Thompson and others worked. Robin Cook MP often attended and he also travelled to Nottingham to discuss matters.

Some real political differences had begun to emerge in the co-ordinating committee. For example, Edward had remarked that there was a 'whiff of Bill Rodgers' about the Communist Party of Italy, after the Russell Foundation, at Ken Coates' instigation, published pertinent PCI documents in the second number of the *END Bulletin* of work in progress. For some years, the Russell Foundation had been working closely with the PCI on the rehabilitation of Nikolai Bukharin, the Bolshevik 'darling' of the Russian Revolution. In 1980 at the Instituto Gramsci, the PCI had organised a landmark conference about Bukharin to which leading representatives of communist parties and others were invited. Eventually, in 1988, President Gorbachev rehabilitated Bukharin. By then END in Britain had long been sundered. The break between the Russell Foundation and the END of the Thompsons, Mary Kaldor and others, which occurred in 1983 after the second END Convention in Berlin, actually proved rather creative in the long run. Ken Coates and Ken Fleet had become joint secretaries of the international END Liaison Committee, which organised the END Conventions, while Edward, Mary and others continued developing the North Atlantic Network and related projects, reflected in a lively publishing programme in conjunction with Merlin Press and in the *END Journal*, edited by Mary.

The Berlin Convention in May 1983 was arguably END's high water mark, anticipating Germany's eventual reunification, much to the annoyance of the Soviet Peace Committee. In 1987, Gorbachev and Reagan would sign the Intermediate Nuclear Forces Treaty, which owed not a little to the pressure exerted by the END idea. As Bruce later remarked, there would never have been END without Ken Coates. Nor would the peace movement of the last 40 years have attracted so much sympathy and support without Bruce Kent.

Tony Simpson

Ken Coates, Bruce Kent and friends at sea off Greece

Riding Two Horses

Glyn Ford

Riding Two Horses *traces the eventful life and career of Glyn Ford, Member of the European Parliament for 25 years and erstwhile leader of its European Parliamentary Labour Party. Ford's leadership coincided with a period when the Left was in the ascendancy across much of the globe. The influence of Europe's Left during this era is examined by an active participant with a unique standpoint: a frequent visitor to East Asia; frontrunner in pushing for anti-racist legislation in the European Union; practitioner of 'soft' power and balanced relationships with Asia and the USA; advocate of progressive science and technology policy; political representative and activist in pursuit of an accountable and democratic European Union. Looking ahead, Glyn Ford makes the case that any prospect of the UK rejoining the European Union will be neither easy nor early. Re-entry will be impossible without addressing the UK's democratic deficit, and will more likely follow the break-up of the UK than forestall it. Yet the UK as a medium-sized nation state is largely impotent without constructive engagement with Europe. We print two excerpts that will interest readers of* The Spokesman.

* * *

The 1989 intake augmented both the Tribunites and the right with the Campaign Group standing pat. There was a new element with the 'Federalist Four' – Ken Coates, Peter Crampton, Henry McCubbin and Ian White – on the hard left, but strongly pro-European. Coates had previously been expelled from the party and had been instrumental in setting up the Institute for Workers' Control (IWC). I knew him from my minor involvement in the IWC and a more active role as a founder member in 1973 of SERA. Despite being let back into the party, there is no way he would have been allowed to stand if Labour HQ had thought there was any prospect he might win. He wasn't the only one. Walworth Road's psephological naivety made for interesting times.

Travels with Ken

The following year Ken and I were to be deported from Algeria after we joined Ahmed Ben Bella's entourage that accompanied him home from Barcelona to Algiers, ending his exile. The Algerian authorities allowed 'the president' to land, but decided the foreigners accompanying him were *persona non grata.* Having been detained for a few hours in the port, we were physically forced onto a ferry sailing for Marseille; one of the more recalcitrant was thrown bodily onto the ship's deck as it pulled away from the dock. Many of those expelled were stateless or had passports from countries requiring visas for France. Luckily, Stuart Holland was with us and he phoned French prime minister Michel Rocard's office. When the ship docked, we miscreants were taken off first, and a team of customs officials (arranged by Interior Minister Pierre Joxe) stamped passports on a production line, giving forty-eight hour transit visas to even those with the most dubious sets of papers.

Ken Coates (left) and Ben Bella (right) arriving in Algiers by boat, 1990. Crowds visible behind with banners were estimated at 100,000 people.

This was not my first experience of Ken's political peregrinations. I had travelled with him and Ken Fleet at the end of March 1988 to the Jerusalem District Court to attend the conclusion of the trial of Mordechai

Vanunu, who had blown the whistle to the *Sunday Times* on Israel's nuclear weapons programme and their hundred nuclear weapons at the Negev Nuclear Research Centre, where he worked as a technician. A classic Mossad honey-trap saw him lured from London to Rome by a female agent, from where he was abducted by the Israeli authorities and rendered back to Israel. His trial was held *in camera*. No one, let alone us, was allowed in the court. After Vanunu received his eighteen-year sentence, we travelled down to Shikea Prison in Ashkelon in an attempt to visit. The prison gates were as far as we got ...

Backward to Europe

Labour sacrificed party for nation, hammering the last nail in its coffin in Scotland; it is unconscionable they could ever challenge the Tories as the party of union. There was a strong left case for remaining in the UK and Europe, but Labour never made it – a class case that pitched the interests of employees against employers, labour versus capital, which would conclude that the best interests of the labour movement were served by staying in both. For Labour supporters, opting for independence from the EU in 2016 would have left Scotland adrift in the North Atlantic with no guarantee Madrid would not abort any attempted rescue.

Four years on, coffled to Britain's other nations, Caledonia has been cruelly dragged from a continental union in the interests of a middling nation state. The very idea that circumstances have not changed sufficiently to warrant a second independence referendum would be farcical if it wasn't so consequential. When the referendum comes, the money will be on leave – and it should be. From an economic and political standpoint, the choice of being an integral part of the EU – one of the world's three largest economic powers – or marooned as a peripheral appendage of 'Singapore on Thames' is not difficult to answer. Apart from the single-currency issue – which should not be understated – negotiations with Brussels for Edinburgh would be simple and quick.

As for Northern Ireland, May and Johnson between them welded the economies of North and South together while simultaneously pulling those across the Irish Sea apart. The surge in North–South trade in many sectors far exceeds any losses across the Irish sea. Northern unionism was politically sacrificed to 'Get Brexit Done', all at a time when Dublin has demonstrated over abortion, equal marriage and the rest that it is streets ahead of democratic unionism's reactionary instincts. 'Rome rule' holds few fears for the young and progressive today in the North. Now the economic benefits of a united Ireland add their voice. With Sinn Fein in

2022 the largest party in North and South, a Scottish vote for independence would see Dublin trigger the proviso in the Good Friday Agreement for a referendum on a united Ireland and the end of partition. Dublin would have to be very stupid to lose. The preparation of a comprehensive plan for unification with high levels of autonomy for education, policing and local government in the Six Counties would smooth an end to partition. Even better placed than Scotland – as German unification demonstrated – with the Northern Ireland protocol Belfast can slip smoothly back into the EU without negotiations. Wales has always been the laggard; Cardiff will never lead, but it may follow. With Scotland and Northern Ireland gone, England's last settlement may increasingly lack appeal, and there are seven EU member states with smaller populations.

Where do I stand? I accept Scotland, Northern Ireland and Wales have the right to self-determination. In 2014 the progressive vote in Scotland should have unquestionably been cast in favour of union and Union. The 2016 Leave vote changed the balance of benefit. It was both self-harming for the English – and Welsh – and injurious to Scotland and Northern Ireland. Now it's impossible not to counsel progressives in the colonies of the English Empire that their interests will be better served by Brussels than London. Some may self-servingly argue Labour can't win without Scotland. For me it's unclear whether there is any prospect of hearing the distant bugles of the Scottish cavalry coming to rescue English Labour's circled wagons any time soon. Even were it true, do we really expect the periphery to immolate itself for a centre that bears responsibility for their plight? That's seeking self-sacrifice of a heroic order.

It may in fact be the case that the best or only route back to the EU lies through the backroads of Scottish independence and the unfinished business of Irish unification – a broken UK glued back together within the curtilage of the EU; unity through community. Like the Panda's thumb, the proof of evolution after all lies in those adaptations that arise from improbable foundations. As Tom Nairn argued in *The Break-Up of Britain* (1977, revised 1982), it would be the very process of disintegration that would offer respair by finally destroying Britain's feudal state institutions and allowing a new politics and polity to be born from the ashes. The wisest choice might be to embrace the prospect and work to ensure Nairn is proved right.

Riding Two Horses: Labour in Europe
£14.99 | ISBN 9780851249070 | www.spokesmanbooks.org

Appointment in Wales

When Richard Fletcher met Bertrand Russell

Tony Simpson

Tony Simpson interviewed Richard Fletcher at his home in London in August 2022.

Richard Fletcher went to Cambridge in 1947 to study natural sciences. Later, he became a research assistant to the distinguished nuclear physicist, Otto Frisch, at the Cavendish Laboratory there. Before Cambridge, Frisch had worked at Los Alamos as part of the team assembling the first atomic bombs to be exploded over Hiroshima and Nagasaki. 'All my life I have been interested in the design of scientific devices,' wrote Frisch in his memoir. Fletcher seems to share some of that enthusiasm for design, although for avowedly peaceful purposes as he pioneered innovative processes, particularly of battery powered vehicles. His long-term collaboration with Mike Cooley and others continues to yield new insights into the possibilities of socially useful production, a concept initiated by shop stewards at the armaments company, Lucas Aerospace, in the 1970s. In his tenth decade, Richard Fletcher's creativity is undimmed.

Fletcher first encountered Bertrand Russell whilst an undergraduate at Cambridge. Russell had returned there from the United States in 1944 when Trinity College invited him to a five-year lectureship. His lectures attracted large audiences and Fletcher recalls Russell's distinctive speaking voice: 'fire, water, earth, air'. With friends, he would walk round Cambridge imitating Russell naming the four elements.

In the late 1950s, Fletcher and his wife, Patricia, were intensely engaged in the mass campaign against nuclear testing and the proliferation of hydrogen bombs, which were vastly more destructive than the atomic bombs used by the Americans against Japan. In 1958, the Campaign for Nuclear Disarmament (CND) was launched with Bertrand Russell as President. In 1959, Labour lost the General Election and the Conservative Government continued adding to its nuclear arsenal as well as permitting US nuclear weapons to be stationed in Britain. Frank Cousins, leader of Britain's largest trade union, the Transport and General Workers, also appreciated the existential threat posed by hydrogen bombs. At the Labour Party Conference in Scarborough in 1960, Cousins, Fletcher and others successfully committed the Party to a non-nuclear defence policy against the public position of its leader, Hugh Gaitskell. A year later in Blackpool, the policy was reversed. It was after this defeat that the Fletchers travelled to North Wales to meet with Bertrand Russell in November 1961.

Fletcher had worked very hard to secure the vote for a non-nuclear defence policy at Scarborough in 1960. He told me:

'We had naively organised this first pre-compositing meeting inside the Labour Party to try and defeat Gaitskell. We didn't know anything about politics. There was something like 90 resolutions in support of CND sent into conference. I knew nothing about these things but I organised the pre-compositing meeting and everybody came. There were all these people: Frank Cousins of the TGWU, Horner of the Fire Brigades. Everybody was there all sitting in a row looking at me and saying, "let's get started!" Fortunately, Ian Mikardo was there. He was a bit more experienced and got the meeting going. One lunatic wanted to attach condemnation of NATO. Cousins said, "if you attach condemnation of NATO, I'm sorry I can't vote for it because I haven't got the mandate from my members". Cousins operated the Union rules strictly and if he didn't have a mandate, he couldn't do it. "So tell me if you want me," said Cousins. "But if you take opposition to NATO, I can't deliver my delegation's vote." This haggling went on for some hours. Harry Crane spoke on behalf of the Labour Party platform. He was constantly trying to steer everybody towards this NATO resolution. He didn't succeed. Mikado pulled out a chair and said "come and stand on this chair, Harry, and tell us what we've decided". Mikado held his hand while Crane read something out. We said, "no, that's not what we decided". Crane was trying every which way because he knew his position in the Party depended on him delivering the goods. Otherwise he'd be useless. We defeated this horrible stroke and the resolution went to conference and was carried. It really set the cat amongst the pigeons. There were American diplomats around. It stirred up a hornets' nest.'

Such was the hornets' nest that the vote was decisively reversed at the subsequent Labour Party Conference in Blackpool in 1961 and Gaitskell won a famous victory.

So, by the time Richard and Patricia Fletcher met with Russell in November 1961, there was a major reversal of policy within the Labour Party. Russell had recently been released from Brixton Prison where he was sent for a week for refusing to promise not to engage in non-violent civil disobedience. In his statement at Bow Street in September 1961, Russell said: 'Non-violent civil disobedience was forced upon us by the fact that it was more fully reported than other methods of making the facts known, and that caused people to ask what had induced us to adopt such a course of action.' Edith Russell was also sent to prison for a week, in Holloway. Others were imprisoned for longer terms.

In March 1960, Fletcher and his colleagues had sent Russell a manifesto for a new group that was being formed in Cambridge. In reply, Russell counselled caution, saying a new party needs funds. It is better to work for the conversion of the Labour Party, said Russell. By the end of April, Russell was writing to Fletcher to say that he had grave doubts whether he should remain in the Labour Party, but he would see what the October Party conference would bring. Fletcher burst into action as the conference approached, as we have seen. Russell invited Fletcher for a thorough discussion, although the meeting did not take place until November 1961. In July 1960, Russell told Fletcher: 'As for relations with the Liberal Party, I think we should support any Liberal candidate who is a unilateralist unless he is standing against a Labour candidate who is also a unilateralist.' Russell understood 'unilateralist' to mean nuclear disarmament by the United Kingdom with no expectation of reciprocal nuclear disarmament by the Soviet Union or others. He urged the Soviet Union and United States to negotiate to reduce the threat of nuclear conflict with a view to nuclear disarmament.

Meanwhile, Russell's relations with Canon John Collins, the Chair of CND, were becoming strained. In particular, Russell was more supportive of those activists engaging in direct action such as sit-down protests, in which he participated himself. In September 1960, Patricia Fletcher sent Russell an exchange of letters with Collins about the Labour Party and other matters. Russell replied that he had 'read Canon Collins letter carefully and I think that *some* of his points are valid. It is undoubtedly true, as he says, that the great majority of the delegates at Scarborough will be mandated already and not open to last minute influences.' Russell added that he was prepared to ignore Collins on direct action – the Canon was not at all keen on such conduct, seeing it as divisive and alienating potential support. On 19 September, shortly before the Labour Party Conference was due to open in Scarborough, the Fletchers sent Russell a 'copy for mimeograph' of what they proposed to circulate to delegates. On 29 September, Russell replied to say 'as you will know, although I was anxious not to quarrel with Canon Collins, events have forced a public disagreement on the question of Direct Action. I am afraid this may have a bad effect at Scarborough, which I shall deeply regret.' In the event, the votes at Scarborough in 1960 registered a signal success for nuclear disarmament. Later in October, the formation of the Committee of 100 was announced, arguing for mass civil disobedience to somehow compel the removal of nuclear weapons. Russell put himself at the head of the campaign, supported by Ralph Schoenman. Michael Randle and others, and he resigned the presidency of CND. It would be four more years before Russell publicly tore up his Labour Party membership card, in October 1965, by which time Harold Wilson was the Labour Prime Minister whose foreign policy, particularly in relation to the US war on Vietnam, appalled Russell in many respects.

Russell had counselled Fletcher against trying to set up a rival party to Labour, and subsequently lost patience with the Party himself. Nevertheless, Fletcher seems to have taken Russell's advice to heart because he continued to lobby Labour Party conferences for decades afterwards. *The Observer* newspaper had a 'Briefing' section. Fletcher cut out the banner and used it as artwork for the first Labour Party Conference *Briefing*. Delegates readily accepted free copies that were handed out each morning, which set out the key votes of the day ahead. It was this work at Conference that brought Fletcher into close contact with Ken Coates, who acknowledged Fletcher's organisational flair with *Briefing* and *Voice of the Unions*. In due course, Russell invited Coates to work with him in the Bertrand Russell Peace Foundation. *Briefing* in different guises continues to appear at Labour Party Conferences.

'My letter to Russell must be somewhere in the Archives,' says Fletcher. In fact, there are some 20 items of correspondence between Bertrand Russell, Richard and Patricia Fletcher, as well as Russell's assistants Christopher Farley, Ralph Schoenman and Russell Stetler listed in the BRACERS database of the Bertrand Russell Archives at McMaster University, Canada. They span the last decade of Russell's life in the 1960s.

Workers' Control

Bulletin of the Institute for Workers' Control

ISSN 0306 1892

1981: Number 4   Price 60p

Toxteth, Brixton, Southall:

a crime?

Mike George

1947-2022

Mike George regularly attended residential conferences organised by the Institute for Workers' Control. On one occasion in the early 1980s during the reports-back from workshops, Mike confessed that he hadn't really wanted to give up his weekend for another IWC conference in Nottingham. But, after 36 hours in the company of comrades, he was glad he had made the effort.

There was vitality to those gatherings that built confidence for the struggles ahead. Mike compiled 'Combine News' for the *IWC Bulletin*, which reported developments at Lucas Aerospace, Vickers, Metal Box, Dunlops and other shop stewards' committees. His pivotal role at the Centre for Alternative Industrial and Technological Systems (CAITS) provided a vantage point for this work. Located in Dagenham at North East London Polytechnic, CAITS was the catalyst for much pioneering work in pushing forward the frontier of workers' control. Mike Cooley, who co-authored a notable critique of Labour Party policy with Mike George (see *Planning the Planners*, Spokesman for the IWC, 1983), Richard Fletcher, Hilary Wainwright and others opened up these educational facilities in pursuit of popular planning for social need. In due course, this pioneering work was taken forward by the Greater London Council (GLC), which Mrs Thatcher abolished in 1986.

Mike George's exuberance and candour combined with real political insight, as this article from 1981 makes plain. The Tories under Margaret Thatcher were preparing the ground for a major offensive against the Labour Movement. Thatcher remembered that Prime Minister Heath had been defeated by the miners and others in the 1970s. She was intent on reversing that experience. There are some parallels with current politics in Britain as the re-constituted UKIP/Tory government aligns itself with some train operating companies against the rail unions. However, this time the Tories have imposed on the country a prime minister whose mandate is tenuous and whose competence is open to question.

Tony Simpson

Workers' Plans

What they mean and what they might mean

Mike George

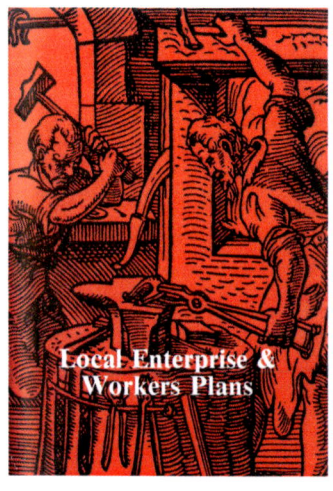

The Employers' Offensive

Amongst many (if not most) of Britain's larger companies there is a new, politically-minded, offensive being waged by employers – British Leyland is only the most obvious example. A couple of years ago the head of STC (part of ITT) called upon employers to mount a *political* offensive in order to curb the power of trade unions. This call has been heeded, for instance over the past 18 months there have been a number of high-level conferences of employers' representatives, all debating ways and means of reversing the supposed growth of union power. A recent conference made it clear that employers expect to have another 18 months or so in which to carry this out.

Obviously the existence of a Conservative Government more radically committed to a free market economy than any since World War II is a very major factor in this offensive. The Tories' adherence to major policy decisions means in practice much more than so-called monetarist policies. Monetarism provides a useful populist approach to the economy – putting it into the realm of 'good housekeeping'. It also provides one of the mechanisms for putting the economy into a political framework which denies power to organisations in society which do not represent finance capital.

This *political* reconstruction of the nature of the economy means that industrial capital – those that control industry must 'shape up' into a more political force which owes long-term allegiance to finance capital. So, we've seen the Confederation of British Industry (CBI) upset over the continuation of high interest rates, the overvalued £, and over the 'market' pricing policy of energy. None of these factors directly aids industry, quite the reverse – adding to industrial companies' oft-quoted difficulties in the current trading recession. Yet many top industrialists declined to support the CBI's position, some even leaving the CBI altogether. Why is this?

It is clear that the Stock Market and other financial institutions have not suffered the decline in confidence which appeared in the mid-1970s, indeed the Stock Market in general is 'bullish'. Finance capital, it is presumed, will be aided by Tory policies.

It would be wrong however to assume that it's only a matter of the industrialists "having to shape up", for there is more than just a coincidence of interests between the Tories and Big Business. Business leaders like Edwardes of BL, Scott of Lucas and Campbell Fraser of Dunlop have operated on the trade unions in a coherent, political way themselves. Trading difficulties are used by them to create quite comprehensive strategies in relation to Labour and the unions. For instance it was *no coincidence* that Derek Robinson was dumped, the combine shop stewards committee undermined, that new working methods were introduced at Longbridge, and that the Mini Metro's 'success or failure' was held up as a symbol of Britain's success as an industrial power. At Dunlop the latest redundancy threat (to 1,800 jobs) is being directly used as a lever to try to reduce the power of shop stewards at a number of plants.

The Tories' philosophy also means a withdrawal of support from various parts of society, including unemployed, sick and disabled people, and urban areas suffering from economic and social deprivation. And no longer is the State employer of last resort, it is one of the toughest employers around now. Obviously not all of these features are completely new (the last Labour Government operated monetarist policies), but the clarity of political will certainly is.

Whilst a change in the 'terrain' upon which Government aid is given to industry remains the main direction of policy, albeit tempered by certain tactical necessities, this is being achieved in a way which integrates well with the Tories' interventions in another part of industry. Conditions are being created whereby one major organised sector of society is being made marginal – because it has historically held a very different view of society and industry, namely the trade union movement. Some of these conditions are being created through direct legislative attacks, such as the 1980 Employment Act, but others are brought about indirectly. The Tories are removing trade union power via the employers. The odd, politically expedient gesture of support for small businesses, or the maintenance of certain regional incentives cannot be read as a 'U Turn'. The post-war forms of political involvement allowed to trade unions, albeit to achieve consensus, are being swept away.

Those employers who understand the longer term aims of the current Tory philosophy and politics can therefore find a happy coincidence of interests! The recessionary trading conditions, the overvalued £, high interest rates are combining to create the need for companies to radically restructure and slim-down their businesses. This is releasing money internally, which is needed to cover overheads (as production levels are cut), and for investment in labour-saving and other new technologies. The 'internal' conditions created by restructuring, rationalisation and redundancy are of course detrimental to trade union power, but many employers are taking advantage of these conditions to directly attack shop floor trade unionism as well.

So the trade unions are facing a many-sided attack. Legislation is curbing many trade union activities, such as secondary action and picketing. Job losses, short time working and closure threats are undermining militancy and affecting bargaining activities. And there is a continuing ideological attack on unions, through the media and elsewhere, which attempts to portray unions as irresponsible and destructive at worst, irrelevant or useless at best.

The sheer size of the labour shake-out in industry has surprised the Tories, but pleasantly we must presume. The Government has had to put millions of pounds more into the redundancy payments fund to avoid it going bankrupt. These shake-outs are on a much bigger scale than in the mid-1970s – when companies' liquidity problems were greater than they are now. Reductions in labour have commonly occurred "across the board", affecting many plants (sometimes via complete closure), and often taking the form of enforced redundancies. The effects of this scale of job losses was reflected in the strike statistics for 1980 (the lowest for decades). Trade unions have 'had to' relinquish many shop steward and other union rights and practices. And as the unions have backed down in the face of job losses so have many employers taken the opportunity of 'explaining' to employees why they must make sacrifices for the good of the company (and for themselves, of course) – often by-passing union channels altogether by writing direct to employees or producing special 'employee reports' on the business.

The companies' lectures on 'business realism' have of course been directed towards wages too, the downwards pressure on wages has been aided by threats to jobs – wage cuts or even bigger job cuts. Companies have been only too anxious to explain their view of economics to their employees during this recession. This has been markedly successful in certain sectors such as engineering and a lot of manufacturing industry. Trade unions have been told that there will be no wage negotiations – for the first time in decades some unions have had to forfeit their collective bargaining rights and functions! Wage awards which go nowhere to meeting cost of living increases have effectively undermined unions' major contribution to the membership – the longer term consequences of this are grim.

Changes in the work environment and in working methods, often via the introduction of new technology, are being pushed through on the back of job cuts and the 'necessary' reduction of labour costs. The most obvious example of this is of course the Longbridge plant of BL – this is being used politically as a symbol of the 'new economic realism', and it's no wonder that BL 'welcomes' Nissan to Britain for it hopes it will bring into the country's car industry yet more changes in work methods. Hand in hand with these new methods is an attack on shop stewards' control, rights and organisation (BL, Ford, Dunlop etc.).

So trade union organisation is being hit by redundancy and closure threats, short-time working and the breakdown of conventional bargaining rights and practices over wages and conditions. Shop floor organisation is in great danger, both directly through curbs on shop stewards, and indirectly through the narrowing of areas of negotiation. This is reflected at all levels in unions, right to the level of the TUC.

In general terms there has been only one major change in the areas of intervention and activity allowed to trade unions over the past half century. Bargaining and related activities over wages and certain conditions relating to employment contracts was joined by participation in indicative planning of certain industries. This occurred in World War II, and has continued (at different levels of involvement and activity) up to the end of the 1970s. Bargaining is under attack, and now, despite the continued existence of the Neddies etc., unions' involvement in industrial and economic planning is also at an end – except in the most formal sense. The trade union movement and the labour it represents is being effectively displaced – in economic and political terms. Large areas of economic (and social) life are becoming non-negotiable. If the Tories have their way trade unions are to become like most other voluntary bodies in society. They will be allowed to exist subject to 'normal' contract and property law, and their sole function will be to provide a certain coherence to what might otherwise be a somewhat too anarchic style of employment and wage regulation.

A Response to the Offensive?

Many people in the trade union and labour movement seem surprised at the lack of militancy amongst those large groups of organised workers who have faced massive job losses, closures, and attacks on trade union organisation and activities. The lack of a believable alternative to fight for must figure largely in this, for without a clear aim the trade union and labour movement has few effective weapons to fight the many-sided employers' offensive.

"But", some would argue, "we've got an alternative, it's the Alternative Economic Strategy". In some ways it certainly *is* an alternative, for it proposes that we spend our way out of recession through a £6bn increase in public spending, and it's presumed that some of the jobs will come back – directly in the public sector, and indirectly through increased spending and therefore home demand for goods. It tackles the imports 'problem' by calling for planned trade. It demands that some exchange control measures be introduced in order that capital outflows from the UK can be curbed. It proposes new Planning Agreements in companies, which will integrate into national economic planning. It raises again the use of Price Controls.

But it also demands more Government aid to industry, and a lot more money to be put into job creation-type schemes for the unemployed. It proposes a new National Investment Bank to back up a reconstituted National Enterprise Board.

There are many detailed arguments around each of the points in the Alternative Economic Strategy and there's not space here to explore them. However there are a few matters which should be considered which are in the end crucial to the question of whether this really *is* a viable alternative.

Firstly it doesn't mention anything about *how* these measures are to be effected, and that's because it's assumed that it's simply a matter of having a Left Labour Government in power. This assumption was made in 1973 and 1974, and look what happened: all the rhetoric remained but none of the measures were carried out, except in the most formal, 'top-down' manner. All the Civil Service power, all the *managerial* Neddie-type bodies were unchanged – Planning Agreements foundered and the NEB became a merchant bank. The fact that certain trade union leaders served on the many planning and other industry bodies made not one jot of difference; the bodies themselves worked on the battle of the employers' interests, and trade unionists were nearly always in the minority on these bodies anyway.

It's no accident that there's nothing in the Alternative Economic Strategy about this. For if you look at it closely it is firmly based on the assumption that workers can *only* pursue their interests within an expanding and productive private company sector. The only claim made on the employers' power is that they sit round tables discussing with trade unionists and Government representatives ways and means of increasing efficiency and competitiveness. The Planning Agreements, planned trade and exchange control measures will be applied *within* this framework of business efficiency, for despite various statements about trade union involvement at national and shop floor level there is no clear statement about any possible conflict of interests. If you will recall, exactly the same sort of vague commitment to democracy in Planning Agreements was evident in Labour's 1974 programme.

On this basis the Alternative Economic Strategy looks very much like a straightforward return to Labour's Industrial Strategy as pursued in 1974-1979, and we all know that that did nothing to aid the 'irreversible shift' of power to working people. In that time company taxation became a joke, with all major manufacturing companies being relieved of the duty to pay tax (in effect), and companies got £10 millions a week of public money through the Industry Acts – with little or no discernible benefit to workers. There's nothing said about tax now, and the proposal is to give yet more public money to companies with no trade union or public accountability over its use (which in many instances is supposed to create jobs).

It has been said that the last Labour Government's Alternative Economic Strategy (the basis of the present one) had the political advantage that it commanded popular support (right up to the day of the election). But is this so? Over 20 trade union organisations directly affected by the Strategy, and representing perhaps 100,000 or so workers, have recently collaborated on a book* which condemns Labour's strategy – and this is only the tip of the iceberg. Another way of looking at this 'popular support' is that it formed the cement of the Social Contract, and bought a few years' consensus between Government and trade union leaderships. Few would deny that a certain degree of consensus might at times be necessary or useful, but that consensus was then and is now based upon a managerialist view of industry and the economy in which workers' only involvement is in the form of 'lobby fodder'.

What is also very evident is the fact that the Alternative Economic Strategy ignores the employers' current offensive. It provides nothing for today's struggle, just a set of outline policies for the future, and the

---

* *State Intervention in Industry: A Workers' Inquiry*, Coventry, Liverpool, Newcastle and N. Tyneside Trades Councils, Spokesman, 1982

political struggle is actually an 'internal' one in the Labour Party and certain unions over the precise form of these policies, not actually a political struggle against the forces and agents of the current offensive against the trade union and labour movement. This is not to deny the need for political struggle within the organisations of the labour movement, but it *is* crucial to recognise that this form of politics has done nothing to reverse the erosion of trade union and labour rights. If the employers' offensive is not checked and reversed the operation of the Alternative Economic Strategy will occur in a situation where workers and their representatives have been thoroughly beaten down – this would hardly be a situation which would ensure that the Strategy is operated in the interests of workers (surely history has taught us that!)

This brief and, some might think, rather brutal attack on the Alternative Economic Strategy, is not designed to destroy its credibility completely, for certain elements, like increased public spending would have to be defended. It should however help to show that it is not *the* alternative to fire and mobilise the trade union and labour movement against current policies and practices (Government and employers) and for a real alternative to unemployment and the rest. Some of its 'empty boxes' don't look too bad, but what goes into them must unequivocally be *our* proposals and demands, not the country's managerial elite.

Workers' Plans

The current employers' offensive should be looked at squarely, for the trade union and labour movement has much to learn from it, and not to do this simply engenders defeatism and a lack of informed industrial and political action. How the fight against the employers' offensive is mounted *now* could have profound implications for future industrial and economic strategies.

Workers' Plans are not simply about socially useful products, they represent workforce and community initiatives which are truly *independent* of the managerialist framework of industrial and economic decision-making and analysis.

They are about (i) seeking appropriate and effective forms of union organisation to deal with vastly changed corporate structures, (ii) using knowledge and information obtained through the labour process for the purposes of getting a handle on those corporate decisions which affect jobs and other employment matters, (iii) using this knowledge and information to build up an *independent* bargaining position based firmly on the workers' view of what they require from the enterprise, (iv) extending the boundaries of collective bargaining and related activities, not accepting managements' definitions of what is or is not negotiable, (v) overcoming traditional divisions between industrial, economic and social policy, partly through production proposals to meet social needs in communities, partly through demands on company taxation, Government grants and the rest.

These plans have in practice represented effective counters to corporate power, mainly by cutting through the fabric of the employer's arguments about 'necessary' sacrifices for the good of the company. There are a number of examples available, covering wages, new technology, job losses and pensions. In Lucas some 2,000 jobs were saved in this way. The introduction of new technology is being carried out very much under the Combine Committee's terms, these terms are largely embodied in a New Technology Alternative Plan, and a subsequent Model Agreement. Meanwhile work is in hand to prepare a wages claim which analyses the company's 'ability to pay'; with so many companies formally declaring poor results it's doubly important to look closely at their Accounts – Lucas last half-year results showed an apparent profits drop of over 40%, but the real drop was only some 10%.

In Metal Box, the Combine Shop Stewards Committee is similarly considering a 'Value-Added' wage claim, which takes little account of 'declared' profit, and looks instead at the rate of extraction of value from each employee. The Committee has also engaged in a number of advance planning procedures, in which 'getting a handle' on the company's intentions and policies has been crucial in various redundancy and closure situations.

In Dunlop the Combine Committee is preparing a workers' plan response to a current redundancy situation, and has started on a longer term development of shop floor bargaining strategies in relation to new technology – especially in tyre manufacture. There are many other examples that could be quoted, which makes it clear that a growing number of shop stewards' committees do not see their members' salvation in some new version of the National Enterprise Board (NEB) – it couldn't help *now* and it won't help in the future. And this view is shared by a growing number of Trades Councils and other local bodies (including some local Councils) which need solutions *now*.

The Trades Councils are trying to join up to present a unified view on industrial policy, a view which is based firmly on the experiences of a great many shop stewards' organisations in their various areas. Similarly, the Joint Forum of Combine Committees (involving some *15* Combines) is bending its collective mind to the need for rank and file based initiatives.

It is no longer true to say that Alternative Plans or Workers' Plans are isolated 'events', although four or five years ago this would have been true. Experience of Labour's Industrial Strategy, and now experience of the Tories and of the employers' offensive is changing the situation to a point where there is emerging a coherent and substantial trade union-based alternative – both to current economic and political policies, and to the so-called Alternative Economic Strategy.

This alternative is based on:

i. The development of new organisational forms, which are more effective in relation to the structures of large enterprises.
ii. A new approach to getting and using company information, which avoids the 'Catch 22' of normal Information Disclosure provisions – "how do you know what information you need if you haven't got any anyway?"
iii. The development of community-based social and economic audits, which make clear the concrete effects of corporate policies and actions.
iv. The development of Plans for running enterprises in different ways, which are based on the assumption that they should be run for those who work in them and for those in the community that are affected by them.

This alternative can provide effective trade union and labour movement policy and action now against the employers' offensive, but it also lays the basis for a much more radical and far-reaching 'alternative economic strategy'. It doesn't make the assumption that workers' interests can *only* be met via a conventionally profitable and competitive private sector, it doesn't assume that the State will provide all, via its tie-up with big business. Rather it assumes that future industrial policy or strategy should be based squarely on the interests and the initiatives of those who are most directly affected by those policies and strategies – workforces and their communities.

What is being said is that working people *are* quite capable of determining industrial policy, and by implication other policies, such as those relating to the operation of nationalised industries, public corporations, the NHS etc. It is the workers' plan type of educational and politicising experience which will make this real, not forgetting the crucial point that mobilising *now* against the offensive stops all this from being 'airy fairy'.

A new political territory is being opened up – as a result of the frustration and anger of a great many people over what they see as a tired re-run of limited and limiting policy options. They don't want to be offered those nice-sounding but *empty* policies again, they want to put into them policies and strategies which are more than a sell-out. But of course much will depend upon who in the labour and trade union movement will see this energy and initiative as a threat ...

Workers' Control | Books and Pamphlets

A large selection of books and pamphlets, published by the Institute for Workers' Control and Spokesman Books, is available to buy or download from our websites:

www.spokesmanbooks.com (pdf downloads)
www.spokesmanbooks.org (to buy)

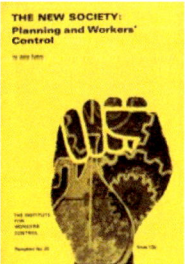

Fates worse than Death

Kurt Vonnegut Jr.

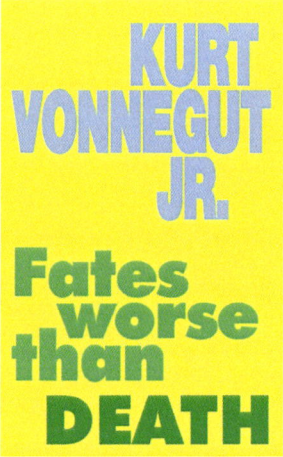

In Kurt Vonnegut's centenary year, we recall his long and active engagement with the Russell Foundation, which commenced when Ken Coates invited him to the first END Convention in Brussels in 1982.

Foreword

A little over two years ago, the Russell Foundation launched an Appeal for European Nuclear Disarmament. We were scared. The arms race was running wild, and the big nuclear powers were threatening each other as if the next war were going to be fought with catapults. Thousands of people agreed with our Appeal, and signed it. Among them was Kurt Vonnegut Jnr, who knows about war at first hand because he was a prisoner of war in Dresden when allied bombers burnt that city, and almost everyone in it.

For two years now, we have been trying to organise a European Conference of all the disarmament movements. At last this is scheduled to meet in Brussels, on 2nd, 3rd and 4th July 1982. After that, we hope to move in to a second big conference in Berlin during 1983.

I think these meetings will succeed. They have to succeed, because the peace movements absolutely have to speak to one another, exchange ideas, learn to share each other's experiences, problems and successes.

But in one way, however many people come to Brussels, the END Convention is already a great success. And that is because of Kurt Vonnegut. I wrote to him to ask him for a message to the Convention. In fact, I wrote more than once, but in the end he replied. This is what he said:

2 June 1982

Dear Ken Coates,
I'm sorry to have been such a slovenly responder to your good letters. I can't

come to Brussels in July, but the world seems to be one big city now. I ran into the Mayor of Nagasaki, whose mother was pregnant with him when the bomb was dropped, only this afternoon – two hundred yards from my doorstep. As it turns out, he is for peace. Surprise.

I, a druid, preached for peace at the Episcopal Cathedral here, St. John the Divine, two Sundays ago. I enclose a copy of what I said, more or less. If anything in it is of any use to you, please help yourself. The copyright is owned by the Cathedral, which paid me zero. They wouldn't have the balls to sue, no matter what you did.

Cheers
Kurt Vonnegut

The piece he sent is a gem. Opening that letter was nicer than being given a parcel of diamonds as big as marbles. In the middle of the Falklands war, with people dying and threatened with death, this is the finest message we could have had for the delegates to the Brussels meeting.

Ken Coates

* * *

Fates worse than Death

Kurt Vonnegut
Lecture at St. John the Divine. NYC
23 May 1982

Good morning,
This is a pretty small church, but I guess I have to start somewhere.

Actually, this is not my main line of work. Preaching in Cathedrals is just a hobby. I make up stories for a living. I get my ideas from dreams.

The wildest dream I have had so far is about *The New Yorker Magazine*. In this dream, the magazine has published a three–part essay by Jonathan Schell, which proves that life on Earth is about to end. I am supposed to go to the largest Gothic cathedral in the world, where all the people are waiting, and say something wonderful – right before a hydrogen bomb is dropped on the Empire State Building.

People as far away as Bridgeport will die instantly.

Here is how I interpret the dream: I consider myself an important writer, and I think *The New Yorker* should be ashamed that it has never published me.

* * *

I will speak today about the worst imaginable consequences of doing without hydrogen bombs. This should be a relief. I am sure you are sick and tired of hearing how all living things sizzle and pop inside a radioactive fireball. We have known that for more than a third of this century – ever since we dropped an atom bomb on the yellow people of Hiroshima. They certainly sizzled and popped.

After all is said and done, what was that sizzling and popping, despite the brilliant technology which caused it, but our old friend death? Let us not forget that Saint Joan of Arc was made to sizzle and pop in old times with nothing more than firewood. She wound up dead. The people of Hiroshima wound up dead. Dead is dead.

Scientists, for all their creativity, will never discover a method for making people deader than dead. So if some of you are worried about being hydrogen-bombed, you are merely fearing death. There is nothing new in that. If there weren't any hydrogen bombs, death would still be after you. And what is death but an absence of life? That's all it is. That is all it ever can be.

Death is nothing. What is all this fuss about?

* * *

Let us "up the ante", as gamblers say. Let us talk about fates worse than death. When the Reverend Jim Jones saw that his followers in Guyana were facing fates worse than death, he gave them KoolAid laced with cyanide. If our government sees that we are facing fates worse than death, it will shower our enemies with hydrogen bombs, and then we will be showered in turn. There will be plenty of Kool–Aid for everyone, in a manner of speaking, when the right time comes.

What will the right time look like?

I will not waste your time with trivial fates, which are only marginally worse than death. Suppose we were conquered by an enemy, for example, who didn't understand our wonderful economic system, and so Braniff Airlines and International Harvester and so on all went bust, and millions of Americans who wanted to work couldn't find any jobs anywhere. Or suppose we were conquered by an enemy who was too cheap to take good care of children and old people. Or suppose we were conquered by an enemy who wouldn't spend money on anything but weapons for World War Three. These are all tribulations we could live with, if we had to – although God forbid.

But suppose we foolishly got rid of our nuclear weapons, our Kool–Aid, and an enemy came over here and crucified us. Crucifixion was the most painful thing which the ancient Romans ever found to do to anyone. They knew as much about pain as we do about genocide. They sometimes crucified hundreds of people at one time. That is what they did to all the survivors of the army of Spartacus, which was composed mostly of escaped slaves. They crucified them all. There were several miles of crosses.

If we were up on crosses, with nails through our feet and hands, wouldn't we wish that we still had hydrogen bombs, so that life could be ended everywhere? Absolutely.

We know of one person who was crucified in olden times, who was supposedly as capable as we or the Russians are of ending life everywhere. But he chose to endure agony instead. All he said was, "Forgive them, Father – they know not what they do."

He let life go on, as awful as it was for him, because here we are, aren't we?

But he was a special case. It is unfair to use Jesus Christ as an exemplar of how much pain and humiliation we ordinary human beings should put up with before calling for the end of everything.

*   *   *

I don't believe that we are about to be crucified. No potential enemy we now face has anywhere near enough carpenters. Not even the Pentagon at budget time has mentioned crucifixion. I am sorry to have to put that idea into their heads. I will have only myself to blame if, a year from now, the Joint Chiefs of Staff testify under oath that we are on the brink of being crucified.

But what if they said, instead, that we would be enslaved if we did not appropriate enough money for weaponry? That could be true. Despite our world–wide reputation for sloppy workmanship, wouldn't some enemy get a kick out of forcing us into involuntary servitude, buying and selling us like so many household appliances or farm machines or inflatable erotic toys?

And slavery would surely be a fate worse than death. We can agree on that, I'm sure. We should send a message to the Pentagon: "If Americans are about to become enslaved, it is Kool–Aid Time."

They will know what we mean.

* * *

Of course, at Kool–Aid time all higher forms of life on Earth, not just us and our enemies, will be killed. Even those beautiful and fearless and utterly stupid sea birds, the blue–footed boobies of the Galapagos Islands, will die, because we object to slavery.

I have seen those birds, by the way – up close. I could have unscrewed their heads, if I wanted to. I made a trip to the Galapagos Islands two months ago – in the company of, among other people, Paul Moore, the bishop of this very cathedral.

That is the sort of company I keep these days – everything from bishops to blue–footed boobies. I have never seen a human slave, though. But my four great–grandfathers saw slaves. When they came to this country in search of justice and opportunity, there were millions of Americans who were slaves.

* * *

The equation which links a strong defence posture to not being enslaved is laid down in that stirring fight song, much heard lately, "Rule Britannia". I will sing the equation:

"Rule, Britannia, Britannia rule the waves"

That, of course, is a poetic demand for a navy second to none. The next line explains why it is essential to have a navy that good:

"Britons never, never, never shall be slaves."

It may surprise some of you to learn what an old equation that is. The Scottish poet who wrote it, James Thomson, died in 1748 – one quarter of a century before there was such a country as the United States of America. Thomson promised Britons that they would never be slaves at a time when the enslavement of persons with inferior weaponry was a respectable industry. Plenty of people were going to be slaves, and it would serve them right, too – but Britons would not be among them.

So that isn't really a very nice song. It is about not being humiliated which is all right. But it is also about humiliating others, which is not a moral thing to do. The humiliation of others should never be a national goal.

There is one poet who should have been ashamed of himself.

* * *

If the Soviet Union came over here and enslaved us, it wouldn't be the first time Americans were slaves. If we conquered the Russians and enslaved them, it wouldn't be the first time Russians were slaves.

And the last time Americans were slaves, and the last time Russians were slaves, they displayed astonishing spiritual strengths and resourcefulness. They were good at loving one another. They trusted God. They discovered in the simplest, most natural satisfactions, reasons to be glad to be alive. They were able to believe that better days were coming in the sweet by–and–by. And here is a fascinating statistic: they committed suicide less often than their masters did.

So Americans and Russians can both stand slavery, if they have to – and still want life to go on and on.

Could it be that slavery isn't a fate worse than death. After all, people are tough, you know? Maybe we shouldn't send that message to the Pentagon – about slavery and Kool–Aid time.

* * *

But suppose enemies came ashore in great numbers, because we lacked the means to stop them, and they pushed us out of our homes and off our ancestral lands, and into swamps and deserts. Suppose that they even tried to destroy our religion, telling us that our Great God Jehovah, or whatever we wanted to call Him, was as ridiculous as a piece of junk jewellery.

Again: this is a wringer millions of Americans have already been through – or are still going through. It is another catastrophe which Americans can endure, if they have to – and still, miraculously, maintain some measure of dignity, or self–respect.

As bad as life is for our Indians, they still like it better than death.

* * *

So I haven't had much luck, have I, in identifying fates worse than death. Crucifixion is the only clear winner so far, and we aren't about to be crucified. We aren't about to be enslaved, either – to be treated as white Americans used to treat black Americans. And no potential enemy that I have heard of wants to come over here to treat all of us the way we still treat American Indians.

What other fates worse than death could I name? Life without petroleum?

* * *

In melodramas of a century ago, a female's loss of virginity outside of holy wedlock was sometimes spoken as a fate worse than death. I hope that isn't what the Pentagon or the Kremlin has in mind – but you never know.

I would rather die for virginity than for petroleum, I think. It's more literary, somehow.

* * *

I may be blinding myself to the racist aspects of hydrogen bombs, whose only function is to end everything. Perhaps there are tribulations which white people should not be asked to tolerate. But the Russians slaves were white. The supposedly unenslavable Britons were enslaved by the Romans. Even proud Britons, if they were enslaved now, would have to say, "Here we go again". Armenians and Jews have certainly been treated hideously in modern as well as ancient times – and they have still wanted life to go on and on and on. About a third of our own white people were robbed and ruined and scorned after our Civil War. They still wanted life to go on and on and on.

* * *

Have there ever been large numbers of human beings of any sort who have not, despite everything, done everything they could to keep life going on and on and on?

Soldiers.

'Death before Dishonour' was the motto of several military formations during the Civil War – on both sides. It may be the motto of the Eightysecond Airborne Division right now. A motto like that made a certain amount of sense, I suppose, when military death was what happened to the soldier on the right or the left of you – or in front of you – or in back of you. But military death now can easily mean the death of everything, including, as I have already said, the blue–footed boobies of the Galapagos Islands.

The webbed feet of those birds really are the brightest blue, by the way. When two blue–footed boobies begin a courtship, they show each other what beautiful, bright blue feet they have.

* * *

If you go to the Galapagos Islands, and see all the strange creatures, you are bound to think what Charles Darwin thought when he went there: How much time Nature has in which to accomplish simply anything. If we desolate this planet, Nature can get life going again. All it takes is a few million years or so, the wink of an eye to Nature.

Only humankind is running out of time.

My guess is that we will not disarm, even though we should, and that we really will blow up everything by and by. History shows that human beings are vicious enough to commit every imaginable atrocity, including the construction of factories whose only purpose was to kill people and burn them up.

It may be that we were put here on Earth to blow the place to smithereens. We may be Nature's way of creating new galaxies. We may be programmed to improve and improve our weapons, and to believe that death is better than dishonour.

And then, one day, as disarmament rallies are being held all over the planet, *ka–blooey*! A new Milky Way is born.

* * *

Perhaps we should be adoring instead of loathing our hydrogen bombs. They could be the eggs for new galaxies.

* * *

What can save us? Divine intervention, certainly – and this is the place to ask for it. We might pray to be rescued from our inventiveness, just as the dinosaurs may have prayed to be rescued from their size.

But the inventiveness which we so regret now may also be giving us, along with the rockets and warheads, the means to achieve what has hitherto been an impossibility, the unity of mankind. I am talking mainly about television sets.

Even in my own lifetime, it used to be necessary for a young soldier to get into fighting before he became disillusioned about war. His parents back home were equally ignorant, and believed him to be slaying monsters. But now, thanks to modern communications, the people of every industrialised nation are nauseated by war by the time they are ten years old. America's first generation of television viewers has gone to war and come home again – and we have never seen veterans like them before.

What makes the Vietnam veterans so somehow spooky? We could almost describe them as being 'unwholesomely mature'. They have never had illusions about war. They are the first soldiers in history who knew even in childhood, from having heard and seen so many pictures of actual and restaged battles, that war is meaningless butchery of ordinary people like themselves.

It used to be that veterans could shock their parents when they came home, as Ernest Hemingway did, by announcing that everything about war was repulsive and stupid and dehumanising. But the parents of our Vietnam veterans were disillusioned about war, too, many of them having seen it first hand, before their children ever went overseas. Thanks to modern communications, Americans of all ages were dead sick of war even before we went into Vietnam.

Thanks to modern communications, the poor, unlucky young people from the Soviet Union, now killing and dying in Afghanistan, were dead sick of war before they ever got there.

Thanks to modern communications, the same must be true of the poor, unlucky young people from Argentina and Great Britain, now killing and dying in the Falkland Islands. *The New York Post* calls them 'Argies' and 'Brits'. Thanks to modern communications, we know that they are a good deal more marvellous and complicated than that, and that what is happening to them down there, on the rim of the Antarctic, is a lot more horrible and shameful than a soccer match.

* * *

When I was a boy it was unusual for an American, or a person of any nationality, for that matter, to know much about foreigners . Those who did were specialists – diplomats, explorers, journalists, anthropologists. And they usually knew a lot about just a few groups of foreigners, Eskimos, maybe, or Arabs, or what have you. To them, as to the schoolchildren of Indianapolis, large areas of the globe were *terra incognito.*

Now look what has happened. Thanks to modern communications, we have seen sights and heard sounds from virtually every square mile of the land mass on this planet. Millions of us have actually visited more exotic places than had many explorers during my childhood. Many of you have been to Timbuktu. Many of you have been to Katmandu. My dentist just got home from Fiji. He told me all about Fiji. If he had taken his fingers out of my mouth, I would have told him about the Galapagos Islands.

So we now know for *certain* that there are no potential human enemies anywhere who are anything but human beings almost exactly like ourselves. They need food. How amazing. They love their children. How amazing. They obey their leaders. How amazing. They think like their neighbours. How amazing.

Thanks to modern communications, we now have something we never had before: reason to mourn deeply the death or wounding of any human being on any side in any war.

* * *

It was because of rotten communications, of malicious, racist ignorance that we were able to celebrate the killing of almost all the inhabitants in Hiroshima, Japan, thirty–seven years ago. We thought they were vermin. They thought we were vermin. They would have clapped their little yellow hands with glee, and grinned with their crooked buck teeth, if they could have incinerated everybody in Kansas City, say.

Thanks to how much the people of the world now know about all the other people of the world, the fun of killing enemies has lost its zing. It has so lost its zing that no sane citizen of the Soviet Union, if we were to go to war with that society, would feel anything but horror if his country were to kill practically everybody in New York and Chicago and San Francisco. Killing enemies has so lost its zing, that no sane citizen of the United States would feel anything but horror if our country were to kill practically everybody in Moscow and Leningrad and Kiev.

Or in Nagasaki, Japan, for that matter.

We have often heard it said that people would have to change, or we would go on having world wars. I bring you good news this morning: people have changed.

We aren't so ignorant and bloodthirsty any more
.

* * *

I told you a crazy dream I had – about *The New Yorker Magazine* and this cathedral. I will tell you a sane dream now.

I dreamed last night of our descendents a thousand years from now, which is to say all of humanity. If you are at all into reproduction, as was the Emperor Charlemagne, you can pick up an awful lot of relatives in a thousand years. Every person in this cathedral who has a drop of white blood, is a descendent of Charlemagne.

A thousand years from now, if there are still human beings on Earth, every one of those human beings will be descended from us – and from everyone who has chosen to reproduce.

In my dream, our descendents are numerous. Some of them are rich, some are poor, some are likeable, some are insufferable.

I ask them how humanity, against all odds, managed to keep going for another millennium. They tell me that they and their ancestors did it by preferring life over death for themselves and others at every opportunity, even at the expense of being dishonoured. They endured all sorts of insults and humiliations and disappointments without committing either suicide or murder. They are also the people who do the insulting and humiliating and disappointing.

I endear myself to them by suggesting a motto they might like to put on their belt buckles or teeshirts or whatever. They aren't all hippies, by the way. They aren't all Americans, either. They aren't even all white people.

I give them a quotation from that great 19th century moralist and robber baron, Jim Fisk, who may have contributed money to this cathedral.

Jim Fisk uttered his famous words after a particularly disgraceful episode having to do with the Erie Railroad. Fisk himself had no choice but to find himself contemptible. He thought this over, and then he shrugged and said what we all must learn to say, if we want to go on living much longer:

"Nothing is lost save honour."

I thank you for your attention.

It is 40 years since the massacres in the Sabra and Shatila refugee camps in Beirut, which took place over several days in September 1982. Those terrible crimes, committed by Lebanese Forces with Israeli complicity, have largely gone unpunished although not unnoticed. The memories endure, as Jehan Helou records in her landmark oral history now published in English under the title *Making Palestine's History: Women's Testimonies*. We include Jehan's Preface to her groundbreaking book, as well as an excerpt about Sabra and Shatila from Hadla Ayoubi's testimony. In addition, we republish Tony Simpson's eyewitness account from Beirut, which he visited a few weeks before the massacres. Subsequent events were to prove far worse than he anticipated for many residents of Beirut.

Making Palestine's History

Jehan Helou

Making Palestine's History
Women's Testimonies

Jehan Helou

Jehan Helou was born in Haifa in 1943. Soon, al Nakba uprooted her family to Lebanon. For long years she was a pioneer in the Palestinian national struggle and the women's liberation movement. More recently, her fervour is directed towards children's culture; she is president of the Palestinian section of the International Board on Books for Young People.

Out of the Shadows: Palestinian women narrate their vital role in making history

The history of the Palestinian Revolution is full of leaps and twists, victories and defeats; it has many untold stories, rich and unique; experiences not recorded, and not yet studied; experiences that will disappear with those who lived them. What about the beginnings, sacrifices, the initiatives, the ebb and flow? Much needs to be told, much about the women revolutionaries, who, if they were mentioned at all, it was only peripherally.

The Palestinian women's struggle in the National Liberation Movement is intertwined with the struggle for women's liberation. This book aims to give a voice to those women, the 'unknown soldiers' of the Revolution, with their heroic struggle and bold initiatives. These women were at times decision makers or influenced the progress of the struggle despite the fact they were denied leadership positions.

Few publications cover this subject – certainly not with the same outlook, approach and with an active observer involved. These testimonies are mainly the stories of the Nakba generation spontaneously narrating their dispossession, suffering and heroic struggle. These remarkable testimonies give them a voice not heard before.

As I was part of the Palestinian National Liberation and women's liberation struggle at the time, I believe it is our duty to document this rich experience. The main documents of the General Union of Palestinian Women (GUPW) were lost during the Israeli aggression in 1982. I tried to meet this challenge through higher studies at Birkbeck College, London University; unfortunately, financial and personal reasons halted that. This is how I started to search for other means to accomplish what has become a national duty.

The idea started to grow with me of the importance of recording – before memory is lost and the body gone – the rich and distinguished experiences of Palestinian women in Lebanon, women who contributed to their people's honourable history. The project started in 1993-1994 but was interrupted for personal and objective reasons, and resumed in 2007. I conducted and recorded 53 interviews and had them transcribed. The resulting testimonies were based on personal live interviews, inspired by oral history technique as the best method of documenting the untold part of people's history.

The narrators were mostly women leaders and cadres of the General Union of Palestinian Women – General Secretariat and of the Lebanese Branch – drawn from the different political factions. They were mainly women who struggled at grassroots level and played an important role in defending the Revolution and empowering and mobilizing thousands of women. Moreover there was a very interesting roundtable discussion with women cadres based in South Lebanon about their experience after the Israeli invasion and occupation in 1982. Each interviewee had the full space to tell her story: the process of transformation, personal difficulties and achievements, and her position on related issues of social change. Different angles of broad questions were covered according to the individual's experience. Each testimony is published as told with minor editing to avoid repetition and retain accuracy.

I opted to interview cadres and leaders of GUPW because it covers their grassroots struggle mostly in crisis situations as well as their projects and work among women. Organizational work and political issues inside different Palestinian factions were rarely addressed, though most interviewees belonged to the different groups.

These testimonies formed the book published in Arabic in 2009 by UNESCO through the Palestinian Women's Research and Documentation Center in the Occupied Palestinian Territory. The book was launched in Palestine, Lebanon and Jordan and was well reviewed in Arabic newspapers. Extracts were translated and published in English

I personally conducted all interviews. I was part of the struggle on both grassroots and leadership levels and I knew most of the interviewees and could check the accuracy of the information. This facilitated the interviewees' quick response and cooperation. I thank them wholeheartedly for their willing cooperation and warm encouragement that provided me with the incentive to complete the work despite tremendous difficulties.

Publishing this English edition has been a long and thorny task. Translating from colloquial Arabic was demanding and needed to be checked thoroughly before the draft was sent to a patient and professional editor. The translation took two years to prepare. This English edition is based on the Arabic one and includes 17 of the most important testimonies. It is edited to keep answers as narrated (my questions and unnecessary details omitted) with further work by a professional editor. A short profile introducing each interviewee is included. There are excerpts from three important testimonies by leading women whose experiences in the struggle have been published by others. It was vital to include the testimony of the Director of the GUPW Institute for the Children of Martyrs (BAS) for its richness.

We hope this book will become part of the literature recording the international heritage of national liberation movements and women's liberation struggles. It is a rich resource for research and analysis. I genuinely hope this book will motivate research centres to support further studies of the various aspects of this rich experience of Palestinian women.

Jehan Helou, February 2022
[First published as the Preface to *Making Palestine's History*]

* * *

In this short extract, the lawyer Hadla Ayoubi (1940-2018) describes some of the horrors of the Sabra/Shatila massacre.

Entering Sabra and Shatila

When I and my colleague Wijdan Siyam entered Sabra and Shatila with the International Committee of the Red Cross (ICRC) immediately after the massacre, the dead bodies were still on the ground. We went on the third day. The representative accompanying us advised us not to get too close, saying 'what you see will live with you for the rest of your lives'. We saw from afar and saw enough to send us both into shock.

People persevered. They returned to the camp. Imagine, before sunset they would not go out of their homes – even if a cat moved outside they would not go out. They lived in terror, but despite that they would not leave the camp because part of the plan of the Lebanese Forces was for them to leave Lebanon. Even those who left for just two or three days, some to the Red Cross in Ras Beirut, returned – they all returned. They wanted to keep their identity and, in any case, where would they go? They wanted to preserve what they had. The Gaza Hospital was no longer a hospital. Displaced Palestinian families and Lebanese lived there – Lebanese people in the camp were also killed.

We opened our centres and put the Red Cross sign over the Gaza Hospital. The Red Cross representative installed a communications system with the Hamra office for immediate notification of any events. There were two operators of the wireless system. Following the massacre, on at least half a dozen occasions, people would suddenly cry: 'The Lebanese Forces are here,' and they would run away from the camp in fear. One morning I was going to Gaza Hospital with a representative from the ICRC, a young Dutch volunteer, and a young Lebanese woman. As we stood there someone shouted: 'the Lebanese Forces have arrived'. I cannot describe the scene of people running — you know how sheep run when they are taken for slaughter. The Red Cross representative told me to take the young women and run. We ran, and the people ran, but the ICRC representative stayed. When we got to the end of the camp we waited outside. After half an hour they announced that it had been a false alarm.

Afterwards, the Red Cross representative told me he would have been among the first to be killed, since he had lost his identification card and had no proof that he was a Red Cross representative. We cleaned the Gaza Hospital from end to end and the staff returned to work, gradually regaining confidence, and we re-opened all our centres. Thank God, we had support from people around the world, some of whom would come and visit us. I was extremely affected by this.

I wanted so much to stay in Lebanon but, unfortunately, I have a Jordanian passport and my residence permit had expired and the Lebanese authorities would not renew it. So I had to leave Lebanon. By then I was in a state of collapse. I had done what I had to do during those events.

* * *

Making Palestine's History
Women's Testimonies
£14.99 | 238 Pages | Paperback | ISBN 9780851249056
www.spokesmanbooks.org

Eyewitness in Beirut

Tony Simpson

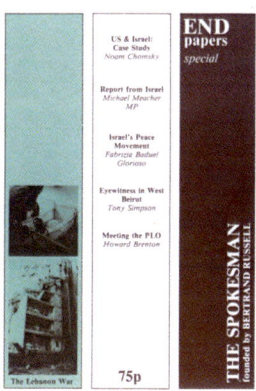

Tony Simpson visited Beirut in August 1982 as part of a delegation of European Young Socialists. This account of his visit, a few weeks before the massacres at Sabra and Shatila, was first published in a special edition of END Papers.

Israel's search for a military 'solution' in West Beirut, now stepped up drastically, has been underway for some weeks in the Lebanon war. Their efforts against the besieged city have escalated recently in a further attempt to break the spirit of the many people still living there. In a war of nerves spun out over many days, military actions are mixed with disruptive electricity cuts, which in turn jeopardise water supplies. Worst of all, regular aid raids terrorise the Lebanese and Palestinian citizens and combatants in the city, as well as the Syrian soldiers who remain.

Yet, as we learnt during our two-day stay in West Beirut, the Beirut blitz and the suffering it entails have far from broken the resolve of the Palestinian-led resistance. Their will to fight, and their readiness, if necessary, to die, make them formidable adversaries, despite their vastly inferior armoury.

We entered West Beirut by stepping under a wire at the checkpoint. No one stopped us, challenged us, buttonholed us, or asked to see identification. Nearby, Israeli soldiers looked on, no badges or emblems on their olive green uniforms, while a lorry-load of French UN forces waited to depart for duties unknown. A little further along the avenue stood a Lebanese checkpoint, and beyond that the first Palestinian positions. We had come to meet the Palestine Liberation Organization (PLO), intending to see how life goes on for the city's several hundreds of thousands of Lebanese and Palestinian residents. Our visit was part of a Peace Mission attempting to increase international pressure to limit further major destruction of West Beirut, and aiming at a lasting ceasefire.

Our party of eight, from six countries, comprised activists in the European peace movements and representatives of several European Young Socialist groups. Sponsored by the Bertrand Russell Peace Foundation, the Spanish Movement for Peace, Democracy and Freedom, and the International Union of Socialist Youth, our mission assembled in the Syrian capital of Damascus, where we met with the PLO and then travelled forwards to Lebanon and Beirut. We also aimed to explore together the wider responsibilities of Europe's peace movements and socialist organisations to campaign both at home and internationally to stop this war.

When we arrived, the war was already assuming genocidal proportions. The battle for West Beirut was claiming vast numbers of civilian casualties. The Israeli shelling of the city began on 4 June, two days before the invasion of Lebanon commenced. Israeli forces swept northwards, probably expecting to take the whole city by mid-June. More than a month later, the city was still under siege. Resistance led by Palestinians, though organised through joint control with the Lebanese and Syrians, was clearly unshaken. Even after seven days of daily air raids by the Israeli air force, with aircraft returning two or three times in 24 hours, bombing both day and night, all thoughts of surrender by the PLO looked out of the question. Rather, the will to fight on seemed to be strengthening. We were left in no doubt that the PLO were willing to die if need be.

There are two halves to besieged West Beirut. One is bustling, noisy, heavily populated and was, until very recently, fairly safe. Together with the considerable Lebanese and Palestinian population who have stayed put, here live the refugees from all over Lebanon who fled before the advancing Israeli forces. Where they can they have occupied apartments abandoned by residents seeking safer homes outside West Beirut. These refugees have been joined by many families from areas composing the second half of West Beirut.

The face of this second half of West Beirut is withering testimony to the immense force of Israeli fire-power, much of it even now still held in reserve. Around the Arab University, and especially in the areas stretching down to the seashore, there are firing ranges for Israel's land, sea and air forces. They have worked intensively. The result is a terrain which looks as if it had suffered a violent earthquake.

Yet many people still live in these quarters, although nowhere near as many as before the siege. In one part there is a street close by some collapsed university residences which most foreign newcomers to West

Beirut visit when they arrive. They have to come here to register with the PLO authorities. You ask the taxi driver for the office of Mahmoud Lebedy, a senior PLO man responsible for the foreign information department. Reluctantly our Lebanese taxi driver accepted this dangerous fare, and sure enough we had to turn back at top speed on our first attempt as the afternoon's air raid came thundering in. Early in the evening we went back.

The entrance to Mr Lebedy's office is reached through a modest bank of sandbags rising to head height. To one side there is an exhibition of some of the shells that have poured down on West Beirut. Their sizes vary greatly. Leaning against the front wall of the building are several bomb cases five to six feet high and well over a foot in diameter. On the makeshift table in front stand a mixture of smaller munitions. As we reach out for the little ones we are warned that the cluster bombs may be live, so it's best not to touch. A walk through nearby streets turns up an abundance of similar fragments, especially the bevelled edges of the anti-personnel cluster bombs.

Organisationally, the city has responded brilliantly to war. Elsewhere in West Beirut, in hitherto safer districts, the Lebanese and Palestinian joint control have worked to measure up to the drastic rise in demand for hospital beds. Dr Fahti Arafat, Yasser's brother, President of the Palestinian Red Crescent Society (Palestinian Red Cross), told us that although they had created several thousand additional beds in temporary hospitals, this was still not enough. The two temporary hospitals we visited, one in a hotel, another in a school, contained both Lebanese and Palestinian casualties. In the women's wards injuries were less obvious, though some elderly ladies were clearly terrified.

Finally our guide, a Palestinian woman volunteer working in the hospital office, took us to the nursery. About a dozen children were there, all in good health, a mixture of orphans from the war and children of the hospital's medical workers. Suddenly, this happy place became a scene of slaughter as the Israeli aircraft roared in and let loose a bomb close by. A second fell still nearer. We ran towards the school's central corridors, thronged with evacuees from vulnerable wards opening to the gardens outside. As we waited to leave, early casualties of this latest assault, all of them children, one streaming blood from her head and legs, were rushed in from cars and ambulances. Overhead the fighters continued to swoop and roar, apparently safe from the barrage of PLO fire. It is at this mounting price in human suffering that Israel single-mindedly pursues its military 'solution' in West Beirut. They talk of plans for evacuation and question PLO seriousness in considering such options, yet the Israeli aim is to destroy the PLO infrastructure concentrated in the districts of West Beirut. Bit by bit the siege pressures are stepped up, ceasefires are called and broken within hours. What will be the conclusion?

Within Israel itself, it seems, opposition to the war is running at a high level. Although they are obviously not yet effective in restraining Mr Begin's military 'solution', 'Peace Now', 'Campaign to Stop the War in the Lebanon', and other oppositional groups in Israel need international support and encouragement. With this in mind, a second limb of our Middle East Peace Mission travelled directly to Tel Aviv, to explain the aims of our visit to the Israeli peace movement.

Internationally, the Habib shuttle has made possible talk of a 'diplomatic' solution, while the casualty lists rapidly lengthen as the military 'solution' is pressed forward. The PLO are most bitter about the lack of support from the Arab world, especially the absence of any moves to apply sanctions to the US, at whose door they lay ultimate blame for the war.

The ultimate opposition to Israel's military offensive in West Beirut lies with the PLO themselves, and particularly with the resistance and civilians who are under siege. Though tense, they were not intimidated by the bombardments. They are proud of their long resistance against all the military odds, and even optimistic that something good might come from this impasse. Possibly there might be a shift in the American position. Extraordinary as it may seem, relaxing between air raids, the PLO combatants are cheerful and friendly. While we were there they even found the energy for a game of football in the street outside Lebedy's office. We asked, 'will you fight street to street?'. The answer came back: 'No. Room by room'.

Shireen Abu Akleh, 1971-2022

Soldiers 2

because they inch slowly towards their deaths

they are
   slightly, slightly, so very slightly less innocent than you

you, who sitting in a pushchair in Kiev
     felt the petals of awakening life fly off the stem

you, who serving cocktails above the Donbas
   found the cabin gone and yourself grasping at air

you, who nodding on the autobahn, braked
   sideways into flashing headlamps and a screaming horn

oh yes, they are only slightly, slightly, slightly less innocent than you

because they are pushed inch by inch, trembling, praying,
   in metal boxes about to be filled with flame
   in grey fatigues through fields draped with bones
   in metal birds ripe to be blown from the sky

   mumbling, sweating, clutching a photo of a girl
     in Moscow or Kiev, a letter, a lucky rabbit's foot

yes, in whatever manner of coffin we have decided
     to launch them to do battle on the ocean of our raging discontents
       they are only slightly, slightly, so very slightly less innocent than us.

yes, slightly, slightly, slightly
   but so very slightly
 that all the sunlit uplands of our righteous innocence
   can never atone for their pain

and Dostoevsky spoke the truth,
nothing is more foul than that
one should decide the hour in which another is slain.

Ben Thompson, August 2022

Reviews

But who will guard the guardians? *(Juvenal, Roman satirical poet)*

David Caute, *Red List: MI5 and British Intellectuals in the Twentieth Century*, Verso, 2022, 426 pages, hardback ISBN 9781839762451, £34.99, (also available in Kindle edition)

David Caute is a professional historian who has held many distinguished academic positions. A prolific author, he has published 16 other such books, several overlapping with the present one. Since my review remains unpublished, I draw special attention to *Isaac and Isaiah* (2013), showing how Isaiah Berlin intrigued to deny Trotsky biographer Isaac Deutscher a well-deserved academic post. This sort of thing, with its implications, is a major theme of the present work.

Caute has also published 13 novels, some reflecting his historical concerns.

For other reviews, see Alan Judd's in the *Spectator* (June 25, 2022, available online) and a distinctly mixed one, also online, by Graeme Voyer of the *Winnipeg Free Press*.

It has been suggested that Caute's book is a hatchet job on Christopher Andrew's authorized *The Defence of the Realm* (2009). This is emphatically unfair. True, the pair are poles apart in their attitude to MI5, but Caute is evenhanded, with frequent mentions of Andrew, both approving and disobliging.

The book is divided into six parts, book-ended by Introduction and Conclusion, a survey of sources with promise of more released files to come, lists of leading MI5 personnel with some special attention paid to Stella Rimington's (first woman chief) memoir, with corresponding list of their victims, ample end-notes frequently expanding the text, a rich bibliography, and adequate general index. No illustrations.

Caute writes in clear, jargon-free prose, always readable, enlivened by flashes of wit. One piddling point: though correctly indexed as Wal Hannington (CPGB industrial organizer), he twice appears in the text as Val.

From a recorded conversation (September 16, 1959). CIA chief Alan Dulles reports Khrushchev saying, 'I believe we get much of the same intelligence from the same people. Perhaps we should share the wealth and only pay them once', a remark fittingly used by Len Deighton as epigraph to his novel *Funeral in Berlin* - maybe not such a bad idea … The fictions of Deighton and Le Carré have done much to create widespread distrust and contempt for British Intelligence. Deighton in National Service did photographic work for Intelligence. Le Carré has always masked what he actually did in his time there, but his attitude can be gauged by this epigram in the Smiley novels: 'There's a theory in the Service that Etonians are discreet'.

Since there is so much negative to say about MI5, Caute is right to praise them for not employing House Un-American Activities Committee (HUAAC) style persecutions. He notes that 'McCarthyism' is a word never found in its files.

We should also notice the ten years activity as a mole within the CPGB of Betty Gordon who went from flogging the *Daily Worker* at street corners to intimacy with high Party functionaries, resulting in a stream of invaluable information for her superiors.

Readers of *The Spokesman* will naturally look first in the index for Bertrand Russell, There are cursory mentions on pages 14, 24, 32, 225, 271, 347. But the place to look is note 3 to Part One where Caute states 'A curious lacuna in MI5's disclosed files is Bertrand Russell'. The dichotomy between undisclosed and disclosed files is a central issue. Thousands of files remain embargoed. Even Andrew was denied access to many for *Defence of the Realm*. There are other oddities. For easy example, some of Iris Murdoch's dossier is 'missing'. On the other hand, no file was kept on Alan Sillitoe, a 'proletarian' writer if ever there was one, who in *Saturday Night and Sunday Morning* included a friendly mention of Nottingham *CPGB soap-box orators* — John Peck springs to mind.

Another gap that should be noted by readers of this journal is Caute's omission of classicist-communist (until 1956) Benjamin Farrington, whose *Head and Hand in Ancient Greece* was republished some years ago by *Spokesman,* with Introduction by myself at the kind invitation of Ken Coates — imagine the size of his dossier!

Sometimes I amuse myself by wondering if (along with many other foot-soldiers) there was a file on me. I fitted their bill: member of Healy's Socialist Labour League/Workers Revolutionary Party, published 'subversive' articles under my real name. Perhaps I gather dust in some forgotten MI5 corner?

Caute makes what seems an irrefutable proof of basic MI5 credos: class-ridden, manifest in, for example, the policy of restricting low-level assistants to upper-class women. Some high-ranking officials were anti-semitic, leading to persecution of many individuals and going easy on

Hitler. Compared to the unrelenting attention paid to Trotskyists, right-wing groupuscules got little attention, except the moribund British National Party — nothing about neo-Nazi Colin Jordan and National Front leader John Tyndall, who did have some potential for trouble-making. MI5's obsession was always with 'subversion' and its myriad individual and collective cases. Caute devotes specific chapters to writers, artists, musicians, dancers, film-makers — 364 in all.

Another MI5 characteristic was homophobia, especially before the 1967 legalization. This led them to devote particular attention to people such as English Professor Arnold Kettle (who gave the most room-emptying talk I ever heard at Nottingham) and Michael Redgrave, thus giving an unexpected side to the dreaded classicist Crocker Harris in Rattigan's *The Browning Version*.

Mention of the tedious Kettle evokes another memory, that of an uproarious Nottingham talk by Hugh MacDiarmid, Scottish nationalist and author of 'Hymns to Lenin'. Caute devotes considerable attention to MacDiarmid, well laced with this remarkable man's comic side.

MI5 was suspicious of actors, authors, musicians, dancers, and so on. Caute deals in detail with many of those who were dubbed by classicist-wit Maurice Bowra as the 'Homintern'. There is some analogy here with Richard Nixon's advice to some political aspirant: 'Steer clear of the Arts. They're left-wing and Jewish.'

MI5 never did get Trotskyists quite right. Despite Stalin, they remained loyal to the Revolution and its ideology. They posed no threat, never have done anywhere, save a brief period in Ceylon. One of their many futilities was endless arguments about what to call Stalin's Russia, the main rival tags being 'Deformed Workers' State' and 'State Capitalism'.

Caute pays some attention to Healy, for a while leader of the biggest group (SLL/WRP) of the day, but also finds something to say even about the miniscule, totally impotent *Socialist Appeal*.

One mistake MI5 made was to take young student 'Reds' too seriously. For many who joined (briefly) the CPGB, it was more of a lark, a fad, the thing to do. Somebody once remarked of 1930s Oxbridge CPGB flirtations that it was all right as long as you could afford the lifestyle. I expand Caute's brief notice of Kingsley Amis. At Oxford, he became a CPGB member enhancing, after his war service with the Royal Corps of Signals, his 'subversive' image with the publication of *Lucky Jim* — hard to think of a dafter misreading. For a while, he published pro-Socialist and Labour Party tracts. Then, over his later years, he changed into a kind of cut-price Evelyn Waugh, parading extreme right-wing views more absurd than most, along with his 'love' of Mrs Thatcher. What did MI5 make of this? Did they transfer him from left-wing to right-wing suspect?

Caute's opening chapter on MI5 and the Great War rightly draws attention to the concomitant birth of the British spy novel. His leading example is Erskine Childers' *The Riddle of the Sands* (1903), quite the most boring 'home reader' assigned to us at school. Better to go with John Buchan's well-known classics, with Somerset Maugham's *Ashenden: Or the British Agent* (1928), praised by Le Carré as having a great influence on his own novels.

Space exigencies compel huge chunks of the book to be passed over. I chose to highlight the chapters on the CPGB and the Labour Party. Neither Lenin nor Stalin had any hopes for the Communist Party, though some amounts of 'Moscow Gold' found their way to King Street. They invested much time and trouble in the Labour Party, but the latter did not reciprocate. Lenin's attempts to gain affiliation were overwhelmingly crushed, as did an offer to help finance the 1926 General Strike. The TUC and the working class were not interested in Bolshevik-style uprisings, and were quite capable of organizing strikes and other industrial actions without any help from Moscow.

Caute points to the files on Harold Wilson and Michael Foot, and the nonsense about Wilson being a Soviet agent. MI5 eventually discounted this, but only after exhaustive digging for evidence, which says a lot about their mentality.

As an addendum to Caute's superlative book, I subjoin Cécile Fabre's letter to the *TLS* about its review of her *Spying Through a Glass Darkly* by the MI6 ethics counsellor (do I hear Le Carré turning in his grave?) that 'the morality of intelligence work derives primarily from the justness of the cause it serves'.

Doesn't always work that way, does it? Does it ever?

Barry Baldwin

Healthy resistance

John Lister and Jacky Davis et al, *NHS Under Siege: The fight to save it in the age of Covid*, Merlin Press, 2022, paperback ISBN 9780850367775, £9.99

The ongoing struggle of the National Health Service in Britain to combat the Coronavirus pandemic has become common knowledge over the past two and a half years due to its extensive airtime and media coverage. Despite many public expressions of gratitude towards the NHS, such as nationwide doorstep clapping and 'thank you' messages plastered across public transport or shop windows, it's essential that *NHS Under Siege* ensures that the British government's failure to protect lives, and its negligent behaviour towards the service, do not go overlooked. As the UK is still run by a dangerous government intent on privatisation and public sector cuts wherever possible, this book will be well received by those who refuse to allow the NHS to fall into disrepair as a result of these Tory attacks. By retelling the history of the relationship between government and the NHS over the past twelve years, the authors show that the Conservative Party are not to be trusted with overseeing this public service.

From the first page, it is clear that *NHS Under Siege's* primary aim is to buttress resistance to 'the siege', which Lister and Davis describe as the 'real terms cuts to the NHS in England'. Alongside their expert contributors, the authors consistently lay blame for NHS failings on consecutive Tory governments who have under-funded the service and have negligently allowed the country to be thrust into a pandemic without adequate medical preparations.

NHS Under Siege has a foreword by Michael Rosen detailing the importance of the NHS throughout his own life, from small injuries through to an induced coma due to COVID. Rosen makes it abundantly clear that 'free at the point of use' health care is an absolute necessity in the UK, and it should be protected from further cuts and privatisation at all costs. Following this, Lister and Davis' introduction and first chapter ('The first decade of austerity') identify the failings of successive Tory governments, detailing 12 years of their attacks, beginning with David Cameron's arrival in Downing Street in 2010 in coalition with the Liberal Democrats under Nick Clegg. By doing so the authors point out that, prior to the beginning of the COVID pandemic, the NHS was already on its knees as a result of austerity policies and privatisation. Reinforcing their points with key statistics, for example drawing attention to the '9000 "general and acute" beds having closed along with 22% of mental health beds' on the eve of the pandemic, *NHS Under Siege* is hard to disagree with, and it becomes clear that the governing party for the last 12 years are not only incompetent but also seriously negligent.

Lister and Davis highlight and explain each of the current government's shortcomings throughout the coronavirus pandemic. They hold the government to account for their lacklustre initial response to COVID, including their failure to procure personal protective equipment (PPE), failure to lock down the country promptly and effectively, and their failure to protect vulnerable and elderly people as the virus swept through care homes following mass untested discharges from hospitals.

The authors go into great depth exposing the facts and figures behind the government's awarding of public contracts and their wasting billions of pounds of public money on a test and trace system which did not work. They detail how the government repeatedly chose the private sector, despite its failure to adapt to the problems posed by the pandemic time and time again. Boris Johnson's government opted to line the pockets of their own, instead of using the NHS and public health teams, which are more experienced and better equipped to respond to the pandemic. Some examples of these shortcomings include the procurement of PPE, the test and trace system, and the 'NHS App' contact tracing system, which was designed to help with test and trace, yet sent out false alerts to users.

NHS Under Siege should be read widely, particularly before the public's next opportunity to vote in a general election. Even those with Tory sympathies would surely find it difficult to argue against their party's utter incompetence and contempt for the National Health Service, which it reveals. As arguably one of Britain's greatest achievements, the NHS should be protected and developed, and a useful first step towards this would be to read this book. *NHS Under Siege: The fight to save it in the age of Covid* is well informed and well presented. It goes a long way to ensuring the reader understands the ongoing conflict between the government's priorities and one's own ability to receive free health care from cradle to grave.

Nathan Collett

Women of Palestine

Jehan Helou, *Making Palestine's History: Women's Testimonies*, Spokesman Books, 2022, 236 pages, paperback ISBN 9780851249056, £14.99, Kindle Edition £8.99

When Germany lay in ruins after World War Two the men were absent and it was the women – *die Trümmerfrauen* – who, we're told, cleared the rubble and rebuilt the shattered cities. It seems the same happened in the ruined Palestinian refugee camps in Lebanon. Women alone rebuilt Ain al-Hilweh camp, which the Israelis had flattened by massive aerial bombardment.

There's much evidence in *Making Palestine's History* of women clearing rubble, rebuilding homes, digging wells, organising sewers, paving roads and cleaning, cleaning, cleaning. They sourced food, medicines, blood, even guns – thus keeping everything going while under fire from the Israelis, the Lebanese, and sometimes from factions within their own ranks. At one point, it was four young women refusing to leave a battle scene who shamed the few young men left into staying, thereby saving Miyye wa Miyye camp following an attack by right-wing Lebanese Christian militia in 1982. (p181)

Author Jehan Helou, herself a distinguished activist, conducted 53 interviews in her bid to record the crucial role of women in the Palestinian Revolution during the 1970s and early '80s. It is clear that in taking part in the political and armed struggle to liberate Palestine, these women found themselves struggling for their own liberation. Muyassar Ismail documents the change:

> 'As for the age of marriage before the Revolution, it was young – 13 to 15 – due to the large number of family members – often from six to 13 in one family and so the father would want his daughters to get married, enabling him to be free of the burden and responsibility for them ... (the revolution helped) ... some girls reach high educational levels such as doctor or teacher. It also contributed to improvements in the economic situation of the family ... the marriage ages of girls increased to between 18 – 20 years old.'

Shadia Helou records her personal awakening:

> 'The revolution is my life. I became aware with the revolution and I developed

with it. Before I didn't know where I was. It opened up a whole new world, a world related to politics, sociology, philosophy and religion. All my culture was turned upside down. Before I was an ordinary Palestinian girl wandering. I was still young. No, it is certain that the revolution made deep changes in my life.' (p70)

Because these Palestinian sisters stayed out all night with men on operations, wore their hair uncovered, chose their own husbands, and trained as wireless operators, engineers and soldiers, previously conservative parents came round to accepting this and their fellow revolutionaries – men – realised that they were truly equal.

'I was the only woman among 75 men: I took it in my stride. All the training that took place was with the attitude that we were all brothers and sisters in struggle and there was a common purpose. My parents knew ... but did not object ... in fact my mother prayed for me,' says Amal Masri. (p100)

There were no so-called honour killings during this period and one woman sets her dowry at one Palestinian pound. Although they were never previously coerced, we're told, now they chose their own husbands or, indeed, chose not to marry at all.

Lots of the women travelled: some went to Vietnam to learn of women's involvement in the struggle against the United States' disastrous proxy war against communism. Others attended the UN Women's Congress in Mexico in 1975 where they succeeded in having Zionism condemned as a racist endeavour (later rescinded, unfortunately). And, like many of their brothers, hundreds of them travelled to the Soviet Union to receive their university education: all this at a time when their sisters in some other Arab countries couldn't leave home unless accompanied by a male relative. This was happening at the same time as the second wave of Women's Liberation swept over the West led by Betty Friedan,[1] Germaine Greer[2] and Kate Millett.[3]

Most of these Palestinian women are not particularly famous themselves but there are cameo appearances by those who strode the world stage at the time. Leaving Yasser Arafat aside, Palestinian-American academic Edward Said mentors one of the interviewees. Leila Khaled, who came to public attention through her involvement in hijacking planes, and diminutive Chinese surgeon Dr Swee Chai Ang, who testified against (then) Israeli defence minister Ariel Sharon, get a brief mention.

But these unknown women were the grass roots who enabled the

Palestinian Revolution and *Making Palestine's History* provides a valuable resource for those who will study the much-neglected role of women in this period of Palestine's history in years to come.

So the Palestinian Revolution – not usually named as such outside the Middle East – begins with the emergence of Yasser Arafat who gave the Palestinians back their dignity following the humiliation, dispossession and disorientation of losing their homeland to the nascent Israeli state, created by the UN. It is seen here as really having come to an end when Arafat did a deal with the Israelis and relocated the Palestinian Liberation Organisation (PLO) from Lebanon to Tunis in 1982. At that point the infamous massacres in the refugee camps of Sabra and Shatila took place. Israel, then occupying Beirut and Southern Lebanon, facilitated the right-wing Christian Lebanese militias who entered the camps to slaughter the women, children and non-combatants left behind; an appalling event which seared – and continues to sear – the soul of every Palestinian.

It's interesting to note the attitude of the interviewees to Arafat – Abu Ammar. They love and revere him with many a 'God rest his soul', when they mention him but they are also exasperated that he doesn't get it. Amal Masri:

> *'The PLO worked to build female cadres to qualify them for leadership of organisational positions: but the liberation of women was not their concern ... There was not a single woman on the executive committee. Why? We used to laugh about it.' (p102)*

And Hasna Rida:

> *'All the women who made it to Fatah's executive committee got there because their husbands were martyrs, not because they were elected or because the leadership acknowledged their role ... As for the educated men, most of them, with very few exceptions, admired the struggle of the women as long as she was not their wife! This changed over the years ... However, if there had been awareness at leadership level that women's liberation was a priority and a basic right, there would have been more positive outcomes and achievements.' (p133-134)*

Since then things have gone backwards – it is very notable in the photos and drawings of the interviewees only one wears the hijab. In Palestine, Jordan and Lebanon in the late 1960s and early 70s the hijab was not common. It is more than common now. Muyassar Ismail:

> '*Women's situation regressed after the withdrawal of the Revolution in the area in 1982. There was reneging on the reform regarding marriage, and early marriage was practised again for girls and even for boys ... Religious currents and organisations benefited from the setback of the Revolution ... the Revolution had not realised the ambitions of the masses ... the oppressed reverted to religion hoping to find there the solutions to their problems.*' (p90 - 91)

Ironically, perhaps, Muyassar is the only woman in the book pictured in a hijab.

Fadia Foda said: '*I feel sorry for the current generation which is lost between the religious streams that are trying to put them back in boxes.*'

The interviewees, now elderly (or even deceased), are admirable in their devotion to their own long-suffering people, their willing self-sacrifice to the ideology which supports their life's work. Their terminology is mostly rather formal and there is a lack of concern for the personal. At one point a woman mentions that her husband took a second wife. We don't know whether she is divorced or if she remains married to him. It's as if her private life is of no account in the great scheme of things. It makes the narrative all the more poignant when emotions are alluded to – see Shadia Helou's account of own awakening, cited above.

Making Palestine's History finishes with the testimony of the only man we hear from: Kassem Aina. He alone seems to stand back and takes an overall view from a very human and humane stance. His focus in on giving children orphaned by the struggle a happy and secure family life. His feeling for women's position is manifest. He says:

> '*The Revolution helped bring out the capabilities of a woman, giving her some freedom, respecting her as a human being, ensuring she was a partner in the building of society and family. We were all drawn towards political activity; it's a short period from 1970 to 1982, and it's good that these achievements took place. We made it internationally; our battle was not only inside but outside also. I think the Women's Union played a positive role, but it was cut short as a result of the defeat. 1982 was a defeat.*' (p235)

Sharen Green

Notes:
i. *The Feminine Mystique*, 1963
ii. *The Female Eunuch*, 1970
iii. *Sexual Politics*, 1970

END

Susan Colbourn, *Euromissiles: The nuclear weapons that nearly destroyed NATO*, Cornell University Press, 2022, 378 pages, hardback ISBN 9781501766022, £27.99

Those of us engaged in European Nuclear Disarmament (END) rarely expressed opinions about NATO. The END Appeal referred to the North Atlantic Treaty Organisation and the Warsaw Pact in these terms: '... *For at least 25 years, the forces of both the North Atlantic and the Warsaw alliance have each had sufficient nuclear weapons to annihilate their opponents, and at the same time to endanger the very basis of civilized life ...*' It concluded: '*We offer no advantage to either NATO or the Warsaw alliance. Our objectives must be to free Europe from confrontation, to enforce détente between the United States and the Soviet Union, and, ultimately, to dissolve both great power alliances ...*'

It is unlikely that politicians such as Robin Cook would have committed himself publicly to END if it was seen as destabilising NATO. Ken Coates commented that the drafters of the END Appeal had 'sweated' to get the ambiguities into the Appeal so that it could attract broad support. So Susan Colbourn's book affords an interesting and enlightening perspective on the 1970s and 1980s when 'theatre' nuclear war threatened to incinerate Europe. She has combed the official governmental and NATO sources, with particular emphasis on Canada, Germany, UK and US. She has also probed the much more uneven archives of the peace movements in Europe and North America. Unfortunately, she didn't visit the Bertrand Russell Peace Foundation in Nottingham, which holds the archives of the international Liaison Committee that prepared the annual END Conventions in different European venues each year for a decade from 1982, so her assessment of European Nuclear Disarmament is somewhat incomplete. Hopefully, this will be addressed on another occasion, and we extend an invitation to her and other scholars to examine these primary sources about END held by the Russell Foundation.

Dr Colbourn rightly focuses on developments in the Federal Republic of Germany (West Germany), which was on the frontline in preparations for 'limited nuclear war'. Not only were nuclear capable cruise missiles (she calls them *Gryphons*) to be stationed there under the US 'dual track' decision of 1979, but also super fast Pershing Two ballistic missiles, which threatened targets to the East. The US 'Dual Track' comprised preparations to deploy on one track and superpower arms control negotiations between the United States and the Soviet Union on the other. Dr Colbourn charts the twists and turns along these tracks, paying particular attention to 1983, the year the first cruise missiles were scheduled to be deployed at bases in Europe.

It was in Spring 1983 that the second END Convention gathered at the International Congress Centre in Berlin, notwithstanding sustained attempts by the official Soviet Peace Committee to scupper it. Yuri Zhukov, longtime operator within the Soviet Peace Committee, denounced preparations for the Berlin Convention following a visit to Moscow by a small group of the German organisers. Perhaps Mr Zhukov had detected emerging interest in German reunification amongst his visitors. Certainly, this was a prescient theme in the discussions in Berlin, that included Egon Bahr and other prominent representatives of the SPD, which had recently lost power and was reviewing its policy. Petra Kelly of the Greens joined the discussions at the ICC, before taking the metro for a manifestation in East Berlin. Oskar Lafontaine, voice of the new generation in the SPD, journeyed to Berlin from his native Saarland to speak for peace. Alva Myrdal, Nobel Peace Prize laureate in 1982, spoke of the new 'resistance' in her message to the Convention, while Paulo Gentiloni, who much later became Prime Minister of Italy, said the Convention 'spoke for all of Europe'. Many of these contributors are photographed in ENDpapers 5, entitled *The Berlin Convention (Spokesman 44)*. Worldcat records 21 libraries holding copies of the journal, including many in North America.

From the Russell Foundation, we organised a coach of some 50 activists to travel from Nottingham to Berlin via London. Before departure, I recall receiving phone calls from Spain from prominent members of the Spanish Socialist Workers' Party (PSOE) who were travelling to Berlin for the END Convention. In May 1982, Spain had joined NATO, the first addition for several years. The governmental decision was confirmed in a referendum in March 1986. Shortly before this, Olof Palme had been murdered in Stockholm, and then Alva Myrdal died, so that END lost two of its most prominent supporters and spokespeople. Palme had been a friend of Felipe Gonzalez, who was Spanish Prime Minister in 1986. 'Spain was sucked into the vortex of the bloc system, and her neutrality has now been annulled' (Editorial, *ENDpapers 12*). In later years, the Spanish Socialist Workers' Party politician Javier Solana became NATO Secretary General and, subsequently, the European Union's High Representative for Common Foreign and Security Policy. Other Spanish END activists had campaigned for a 'no' vote in the referendum (see *ENDpapers12*).

Dr Colbourn quotes E P Thompson: 'if there are enough nuclear weapons now in Europe to destroy the continent 30 times over, what does it matter if one side can do it 14 times and the other 16?' Regrettably, such a perilous situation continues, although now more dangerously as the Intermediate Nuclear Forces Treaty between the US and the Soviet Union (subsequently Russia) has been abrogated. END helped to establish the context for the INF Treaty, signed in 1987 by Presidents Gorbachev and Reagan, which famously outlawed a whole class of nuclear weapons. My colleague at the Russell Foundation, Tom Unterrainer, regularly revisits these arguments through *END Info*, primarily an online journal, which addresses Europe's increasingly hazardous nuclear situation without protection of the INF Treaty. The imminent upgrade of US Air Force nuclear bombs forward deployed in several European countries, possibly to include Lakenheath in England, adds to the complexity and risk.

Far from NATO being 'destroyed', Finland and Sweden, formerly longstanding neutral countries, have applied to join the nuclear-armed alliance following Russia's invasion of Ukraine. In this perilous world, we need more books such as Dr Colbourne's so that we might begin to have a more comprehensive understanding of European Nuclear Disarmament, an idea whose time has, once again, surely come.

Tony Simpson

END Archives

European Nuclear Disarmament: Bulletin of Work in Progress
Published by the Bertrand Russell Peace Foundation.
12 issues from 1980 to 1983.

The pages of the END Bulletin cover the initial development of the campaign, carry debates and discussions of the time and detail activities across the continent.

A full index and PDF's of all 12 issues are now available at
www.spokesmanbooks.org

END INFO

European
Nuclear
Disarmament

@ENDInfo_
endinfo.net

Expanding Nuclear Bootprint

Published by
the *Bertrand Russell Peace Foundation*

END Info was launched in March 2019 to aid the work of the Bertrand Russell Peace Foundation in response to the collapse of the Intermediate-range Nuclear Forces Treaty and the attendant nuclear risks. The Russell Foundation and *END Info* played an important role in building the 'Nuke Free Europe' network (nukefreeeurope.eu), which brings together a range of peace organisations for a joint campaign to rid the continent of all nuclear weapons. In the following pages you will find a selection of articles from issues 32 and 33 of the newsletter. To receive future issues, by email or post, contact tomunterrainer@russfound.org.

* * * * *

Expanding Nuclear Bootprint

Tom Unterrainer

The potential return of US nuclear bombs to the UK was announced without fanfare and – more importantly – without any discussion, debate, deliberation or the opportunity for dissent within Britain's democratic institutions.

There was no official announcement from the British government. No ministerial statement to Parliament. No press conference with representatives from the US Department of Defense. There wasn't even a distinct press or information release from United States government.

When the government was asked about this development by the Green MP, Caroline Lucas, the Parliamentary Under-Secretary for Defence James Heappey gave the following non-reply:

> *"The is unable to comment on US spending decisions and capabilities, which are a matter for the . It remains longstanding and policy to neither confirm nor deny the presence of nuclear weapons at a given location."*

News of this development emerged only after Hans Kristensen, from the Federation of American Scientists, noticed the addition of the UK to the list of nuclear storage sites to be upgraded under NATO's $384 million infrastructure investment programme. In the 2022 US Department of Defense budget, storage sites in Belgium, Germany, Italy, the Netherlands and Turkey were listed. In the 2023 budget, the UK appears on the list.

Let's untangle this a little. Nuclear developments have almost always operated under a veil of secrecy. For instance, Britain's atomic programme was done in secret, with not even the then-Cabinet of Her Majesty's Government being notified. More recently, the current government announced in its Integrated Review that it would "no longer give public figures for our operational stockpile, deployed warhead or deployed missile numbers".

Secrecy – or, at the very least a lack of transparency – extends to the arrangements under which the United States stations nuclear bombs elsewhere in Europe. The US and NATO have never been 100% clear on the numbers of nuclear bombs stationed under nuclear sharing arrangements.

When asked about the possibility of further US nuclear weapons coming to Europe under NATO auspices, NATO Secretary General Jens Stoltenberg said – in December 2021 – "we have no plans of stationing any nuclear weapons in any other countries than we already have these nuclear weapons as part of our deterrence and that ... have been there for many years."

Stoltenberg's comments have been interpreted as meaning that although Lakenheath's nuclear storage facilities are to be updated, NATO has ruled out the stationing of US nukes for the time being. I do not think this makes very much sense. I would interpret Stoltenberg's comments another way. Throughout, he is speaking as the head of NATO. When he says "we" and "our", he is talking about the nuclear-armed alliance. In this context it is worth noting that the UK's nuclear weapons are counted as part of NATO's 'nuclear capabilities' and have been for "many years". This response from Stoltenberg is typical of the prevalent opacity when it comes to nuclear questions.

RAF Lakenheath was the place where the US Air Force stored nuclear gravity bombs. By the early 2000s, 110 B61 bombs were stored there and US F-15E aircraft were stationed there for the purpose of dropping these bombs on command of the President of the United States.

These bombs were removed – without fanfare – in the later 2000's and it was only in 2008 that their total removal was confirmed. For the first time since 1954, the United States did not store nuclear weapons in the United Kingdom.

It had already been announced that Lakenheath was to become the first location in Europe for the new US Air Force nuclear-capable F35 fighter-bombers. These arrived in December last year. 24 of them are stationed at the base and the US Air Force is scheduled to commence training for the use of the new generation of guided nuclear bombs, the B61-12's in the coming year. These bombs will go into production very shortly. According to Hans Kristensen, these bombs look set for shipping to Europe in 2023 where they will replace the B61-3 and 4's already stationed.

So, it looks almost certain that the US intends to station nuclear bombs in the UK again. This is a major development and one that should be taken very seriously indeed. We are not alone in taking this development seriously: our friends in the European and wider peace, anti-war and anti-nuclear movements are alert to what is happening and they stand with us in our opposition.

Even without the massively increased nuclear tensions that have been developing over the past few years, and which have become even more acute over the past months, our opposition would be sharp.

We know that even in the most stable of times, increasing the US's nuclear bootprint would create instability. We are not living through particularly stable times.

We know that regardless of other circumstances, a nuclear storage site and an airbase for nuclear capable bombers becomes a target for a nuclear strike. We need to make everyone aware of this risk and link it to all of the other very good reasons for opposing nuclear weapons.

We know that every new nuclear development brings with it new risks, new dangers and new threats in local, regional, national and international contexts.

Sweden: Social Democratic Women uphold their 'No to NATO'

Annika Strandhäll, Sweden

Annika Strandhäll is the Minister for Climate Change and the Environment in the Swedish government. She is the federal board chair of Social Democratic-women, an organisation with a long and proud history of campaigning for peace, disarmament and non-alignment. Social Democratic-women voiced strong opposition to government plans to join NATO. Here Strandhäll upholds this opposition and considers what will come next.

After intense and thorough discussion, the Social Democrats announced their decision on the NATO issue: the party believes that Sweden should join the defense alliance. It was an expected decision, but it was not the outcome we Social Democratic-women fought for. If the application is approved by NATO, unilateral reservations against the deployment of nuclear weapons and permanent bases on Swedish territory must be expressed.

Social Democratic-women have made a long historical struggle for peace, disarmament and a world free of nuclear weapons. Our starting point has been that freedom from military alliances has served Sweden well. In the party's internal discussions, we have therefore chosen to stand up for our 'no to NATO'. At the same time, we have said that we respect the decision made by the party board - such a major security policy issue is, of course, made democratically.

In the situation we are in now, it is important to look ahead. We will continue to work for solutions in an increasingly threatening world. Dialogue and collaboration must always be our main tools for creating stability and security. NATO membership and military rearmament must not be at the expense of our pursuit of peace and disarmament, in particular nuclear disarmament.

It was thanks to the struggle of Social Democratic-women that the Swedish government in the 60s chose to phase out the Swedish atomic bomb program and sign the non-proliferation agreement. That position must be taken further by the government signing the current UN Treaty on the Prohibition of Nuclear Weapons. Sweden must clearly remain a nuclear-weapon-free zone, in both peacetime and possible wartime. The possibilities of adopting national legislation against the introduction of nuclear weapons in Sweden should be reviewed. Sweden must also work for NATO to become a military alliance without nuclear weapons.

Furthermore, Sweden's feminist foreign policy must be firmly established and strengthened. A holistic approach must be taken to build secure and functioning states governed by the rule of law, reduce poverty and meet basic requirements such as health, healthcare, schools and education. Equal development assistance is crucial. In order for development assistance to be strengthened, development assistance money must not be used as a reinforcement of the state budget. The money must always go to international efforts, with a clear focus on humanitarian efforts and educational efforts.

Nationally, too, it is important that investments in peace and relaxation go hand in hand with efforts to strengthen welfare, gender equality and the environment. We must ensure that the costs of NATO membership and military rearmament are not borne at the expense of other important policies that are crucial to a sustainable and equal society.

A broad political consensus is needed on these issues. We therefore want to see a cross-party working group working for this in the Riksdag. In troubled times, it is more important than ever that we put peace, freedom and feminism first. This is our common future!

Translated from the Social Democratic-Women website https://s-kvinnor.se/

END INFO: Nuclear Europe

US Nuclear Weapons
Volkel, Netherlands
Up to 20 nuclear bo[mbs] are stored in Netherlands and wi[ll be] 'delivered' by Dutch forces when requi[red]. No other nuc[lear] capabilities.

UK Nuclear Weapons
Faslane, Scotland
The UK housed US nuclear bombs until 2008. There remains the UK's so-called 'independent' nuclear capability, *Trident*, leased from the US. Four submarines rotate at sea.

US Nuclear Weapons
Lakenheath, England
Lakenheath hosted US nuclear weapons until the late 2000s and looks set to host them once more. Lakenheath is already home to the nuclear-capable US F35A aircraft. The RAF will not be tasked with 'delivering' the US nuclear bombs.

US Nuclear Weapons
Kleine Brogel, Belgium
Up to 20 nuclear bombs are in Belgium, which is also home to NATO HQ. Bombs will be 'delivered' by Belgian air forces when required. No other nuclear capabilities.

Key

 Austria, Ireland and Malta have ratified the Treaty on the Prohibition of Nuclear Weapons

 UK and French submarine-based nuclear weapons

 US Nuclear Bombs

 Aegis Ashore ballistic missile system

 French 'Strategic Air Forces Command'

 US hypersonic missiles named 'Dark Eagle'

French Nuclear Weapons: Submarine
No US nuclear bombs stored. France maintains a submarine-based nuclear capability, the 'Strategic Ocean Force', consisting of four *Triomphant* class SSBN's. *Also see Air-based.*

French Nuclear Weapons: Air-based
This component of the French nuclear forces is comprised on land- and sea-based *Rafale BF3* aircraft each of which is armed with medium-range cruise missiles (ASMP-As).

The "worst-kept secret"

In July, 2019, a report by the Defense and Security Committee of the NATO Parliamentary Assembly 'accidentally' confirmed the locations of US nuclear weapons in Europe. A version of the report, titled *A New Era for Nuclear Deterrence?* *Modernisation, arms control and allied nuclear forces* was uploaded to a NATO website. Th[e] report confirmed what everyone knew: that U[S] nuclear weapons were being stored in Europ[e]. Further, the report confirmed assumptions abo[ut] the exact location of the weapons and t[he] numbers involved. As a rule, neither the US n[or]

The NATO Dimension

Approximately 150 US 'B-61' nuclear gravity bombs are currently stationed at six locations in five European states. These weapons are in addition to the 'independent' nuclear capabilities of the UK and France. They are stationed under a nuclear 'sharing agreement' as part of membership of NATO. The weapons are stored and guarded under US command, ready to be deployed on host nation aircraft at US/NATO command. Why is this 'Cold War' arrangement still in place? Following the collapse of the Soviet Union, rather than disband NATO expanded to Russia's borders. NATO has expanded not only in a geographic sense but also in terms of 'posture'. Its stated area of operation now extends from the North Atlantic to South East Asia. At heart, it is a nuclear-armed alliance.

Nuclear Weapons
chel, Germany
to 20 nuclear bombs
e stored in Germany.
with other NATO
ember states, German
craft will 'deliver' the
mbs. Germany is also
me to a large number
US armed forces.

'Nuclear Weapon-Free-Zone' Germany
Article 5, subsection 3, of the *Treaty on the Final Settlement with respect to Germany*, signed in 1990, prohibits the deployment of nuclear weapons in the former GDR. See *END Info 7*.

US Missile 'Defence'
Poland and Romania
There are claims that the missiles used on this defence system breached the INF Treaty due to adaptability. See *The Spokesman* 142 for more information.

US hypersonic missiles
Wiesbaden, Germany
The 'Dark Eagle' hypersonic missile system is scheduled for deployment from 2023. Conventionally armed, 'Dark Eagle' functions as a 'first strike' capability. See *END Info* 30 for more information.

US Nuclear Weapons
Incirlik, Turkey
It is estimated that 50 US nuclear bombs are stored at the Incirlik air base in Turkey. Strategically important and increasingly dangerous location.

US Nuclear Weapons
Aviano & Ghedi-Torre, Italy
Around 70 bombs are stored in Italy. Some of these had previously been stored at RAF Lakenheath, UK, before removal in 2008.

European partners discuss the location of US nuclear weapons on the continent, but the report confirmed the presence of 150 nuclear weapons and exactly where they were stored. When the final version of the report was released, reference to the location and numbers of such weapons was removed. The presence of these weapons derived from an agreement reached in the 1960s and is a relic of the 'Cold War' era. When the 'Cold War' ended, the nuclear weapons remained. Now is the time to demand that all US nuclear bombs be removed from Europe, for an end to 'nuclear sharing' and the scrapping of UK and French nuclear weapons.

Nuclear risks and realities of the Ukraine crisis

Helena Cobban with David Barash, Cynthia Lazaroff and Richard Falk

Ukraine: Stop the Carnage, Build the Peace! Introduction and Policy Recommendations

In March 2022, Just World Educational held a series of eight webinars on the international crisis sparked by Russia's February invasion of Ukraine. The sessions were co-hosted by JWE President Helena Cobban and Board Member Richard Falk; in each one, they conducted a broad public conversation on issues raised by the crisis with superbly well-qualified and thoughtful guests.

The multimedia records of all these conversations can be viewed at bit.ly/JWE-UkraineCrisis. Policy Recommendations arising from these conversations are as follows:

1. Ukraine-wide ceasefire now!
2. An embargo on arms shipments into Ukraine by all countries.
3. Start negotiations now, involving all relevant parties, for a lasting peace arrangement for Ukraine, and commit to completion within six months.
4. Monitoring and verification of the ceasefire and arms embargo to be led by the United Nations and the OSCE, or any other party acceptable to both Ukraine and Russia.
5. Immediate aid for rebuilding in Ukraine, including for agriculture, ports, residential areas, and related systems.
6. Immediate international talks on implementation of 1970 Nuclear Non-Proliferation Treaty, under which all signatory states including the United States and Russia committed to complete nuclear disarmament, and a call for all governments to support the 2017 Treaty on the Prohibition of Nuclear Weapons
.7. Leaders of NATO countries should oppose all manifestations of Russophobia.
8. The United States should give up all efforts at regime change in Russia.

A full report on the conversations can be accessed at justworldeducational.org

* * *

For our March 28 conversation, Richard Falk and I (Helena Cobban) were delighted to have as our guests two very experienced anti-nuclear scholar/activists, Cynthia Lazaroff and David Barash.

In my introduction I noted, "Most people who are under, say, 45 years old have no vivid memory of having lived in a situation of possible war between two heavily armed nuclear superpowers. But this is a scenario that looks very close today." This was thus a conversation we felt it was important to include in our series.

David Barash opened his remarks with a stark warning that many observers might conclude from Russia's invasion of Ukraine that Ukraine should never have agreed, as it did in 1994, to give up its Soviet-era nuclear arsenal, and that therefore, "We must adhere all the more closely to nuclear weapons and if anything obtain even more of them."

He warned that the war could also "serve as a massive impetus for nuclear proliferation in the future, both horizontal, other countries trying to derive a message from this, and also vertical proliferation, with individual countries, the US almost certainly among them, maintaining that we need more and 'better' nuclear weapons. So those of us in the anti-nuclear world have our work cut out for ourselves, perhaps more than ever."

Barash said people should understand, however, that historically, "There are many cases in which having nuclear weapons did not work as a deterrent." The cases he cited were: non-nuclear China sending 300,000 soldiers into Korea in 1950 to fight against the U.S. there, at a time when the U.S. had already demonstrated and used its nuclear arsenal and China had none; Argentina invading the British-controlled Falklands/Malvinas in 1982; and Iraq sending 39 SCUD missiles against nuclear-armed Israel in 1991. Of this latter case Barash said, "Clearly he (Saddam Hussein) was not deterred by Israel's possession of nuclear weapons and Israel didn't do anything about it."

He concluded: "We all have a responsibility to declare a just war against nuclear deterrence, which in my mind is really at the heart of the whole nuclear problem that we all face."

Cynthia Lazaroff started with by noting an assessment former Defense Secretary William Perry had recently made, namely that, "The danger of some sort of nuclear catastrophe is greater than it was during the Cold War, and most people are blissfully unaware of this danger. He said, 'We're allowing ourselves sleepwalk into another catastrophe, and we must wake up'."

She continued, "The US and Russia still possess over 90% of the estimated 13,000 nuclear weapons. We still have dangers that existed during the Cold War, such as the risk of inadvertent nuclear war due to accident, blunder, miscalculation, or mistake. We still have ICBMs on launch-on-warning postures with the presidents just having minutes to decide upon receiving warning of a nuclear attack. And these missiles have triggered many false alarms in the past. Plus, we have a whole host of new dangers that didn't exist during the Cold War. These include destabilizing new weapons and missile defense systems, cyber warfare and the cyber-nuclear nexus, emerging technologies, and more."

She said, "We're in a moment of extremely high tensions, in some ways more dangerous than the Cuban Missile Crisis. And... I'm most concerned about two things. First, we have to find our way to a ceasefire to stop the killing, bloodshed, and immense human suffering. And I'm deeply concerned about the risk of escalation which could lead to a nuclear exchange."

Regarding the risk of escalation, Lazaroff said, "We have both state and non-state actors who could take action that could escalate the conflict, inadvertently or intentionally. We have large numbers of NATO and Russian troops now in close proximity in the region. And this multiplies the risk of possible incidents of escalation. And we have uncertainty about where the "red lines" are for NATO and Russia. There are so many pathways to escalation."

Among the risks she noted was this: "The ambiguity in weapons systems that can lead to miscalculation and escalation such as dual-capable missiles that can carry both conventional and nuclear warheads that Russia is now using in Ukraine. And there's no way to know what kind of warhead is mounted on the missile until it strikes its target."

Turning to the question: "Would Putin actually push the button?" her assessment was, "The probability may be low, but the risk is not zero. And I believe... that the longer this war goes on, the more Putin feels frustrated, pressured, backed into a corner the more he feels like he's losing, the more his perception is that he and Russia are threatened I think the more likely we could see some kind of intentional escalation to nuclear use." She said she did not know how the U.S. and NATO might respond, but that a simulation done at Princeton that started with just one nuclear launch by Russia during a conventional war had "escalate(d) to a nuclear war with 90 million dead and injured within the first few hours."

Her strong recommendations were: "We have to end this war to make sure that we don't have an escalation that could lead to something like this or worse... We need to reduce the risk of escalation. And we need to prioritize diplomacy, dialogue, and negotiations to secure a ceasefire and withdrawal of Russian troops and work out all the points of a peace agreement. To achieve this we need better and more open channels of communication at all levels, diplomatic and military... It's omnicidal behavior to stop talking to your nuclear adversary and words matter. We need to stop the inflammatory and escalatory rhetoric on all sides."

She ended by quoting Dimitri Muratov, the editor in chief of Russia's independent newspaper Novaya Gazeta, who won the Nobel Peace Prize last fall, who said, "Only a global anti-war movement can save life on this planet."

In his response, Richard Falk identified the inequity baked into the non-proliferation regime in the Nuclear Non-Proliferation Treaty of 1970, that allowed only five countries to possess nuclear weapons, while those that do not are left in the position Iraq was in when the United States invaded it in 2003. He concluded that, "Both the critique of nuclear deterrence and the complementary critique of the non-proliferation regime lead us in the direction that Cynthia was eloquently suggesting as the only morally and rationally coherent position, which is abolition."

He endorsed Lazaroff's call for a speedy ceasefire in Ukraine and added, "Once that's done, there is an incentive to once more look around and see what can be done to reduce the nuclear danger. And I think... that we need the language of elimination and abolition."

He also underscored Lazaroff's stress on the importance of rhetoric. Just two days before our session, Pres. Biden stated in Poland that Putin "cannot remain in power." U.S. officials tried to walk back that rhetoric, but widespread suspicion remained that Biden indeed entertained an ambition to achieve regime change in Russia.

In our session, Falk termed Biden's rhetoric "inflammatory" and added: "He even hinted at regime change as a goal. Not only does that increase nuclear risks and nuclear dangers, but it also is a guaranteed way of prolonging the war, and fighting metaphorically till the last Ukrainian in order to satisfy these geopolitical objectives... Having a leader like Putin in Moscow and a leader like Biden in Washington and their interaction to me is one of the salient dangers."

* * *

The conversation that followed ranged over a number of issues including:

x the very risky fact that there is much less communication between Washington and Moscow today than there was in the 1980s;

x the erosion of the global "security architecture" that had been built up during the pre-1990 Cold War, including through steps Washington took after 2000 to abrogate treaties like the AntiBallistic Missile Treaty and the Intermediate Nuclear Forces

Treaty and through Pres. Putin's decision in 2015 to cancel what bilateral nuclear cooperation remained;

x more on the riskiness of Pres. Biden's hawkishness;

x the consequences of the United States' failure to publicly adopt a posture of "No First Use"; and

x the importance of working to maintain people-to-people (as well as military-to-military) contacts between Americans and Russians.

What follows is a rough guide to some of what
we said.

* * *

At one point, I asked David Barash how we should look at the risks of nuclear-relevant miscommunication and accident. He replied: "My immediate reaction is to say we should look at these risks with enormous fear and trembling."

He noted that his wife was a prominent member of International Physicians for the Prevention of Nuclear War, a group with members in Russia, the U.S., and other countries, and said: "IPPNW people say there is no communication of the sort that was going on during the 1980s. My understanding is there is no comparable communication going on between highranking US military officers and those of Russia... Certainly with regard to communication, I would have to say things are worse than they were in the 1980s."

Later, Cynthia Lazaroff noted that Defense Secretary Lloyd Austin and JCS Chairman Mark Milley reportedly had tried to contact their counterparts in Moscow, but were met with no response. She noted that, "The longer this war goes on, the risk of escalation goes on, and I think increases... I would like to hear Biden calling every day for a ceasefire. I would like to be hearing him using the words. 'We need a peace agreement. We need to end this war.' I'm not hearing that kind of language."

Cynthia Lazaroff talked about the setbacks she has suffered recently in the efforts she has pursued since the 1970s to conduct people-to-people diplomacy with Russian counterparts. She said that one project she is involved with, to bring together young and Indigenous people from each side of the Bering Strait, had already suffered long delays because of Covid, and now might need even more postponing. But she noted that a Soviet-era (then Russian) general with whom she worked, Gen. Maslin, had told her shortly before his recent death that "If there are young people still thinking about improving relations in the Bering Strait and coming together from our two countries, all hope is not lost."

She commented, "We have to really make those contacts robust again. We have to get different kinds of people collaborating...Climate scientists! We have such a potential for cooperation, and it seems so idealistic to talk about it right now, but I think the work has never been more important."

Lazaroff talked about the importance of the Treaty on the Prohibition of Nuclear Weapons, which was adopted by a number of (non-nuclear) nations in 2017. She described it as "a response to the injustices of the nonproliferation regime and the way the NPT has not fulfilled what it originally said it was going to do in Article Six, which is to... achieve eventual, total and complete disarmament. And the Treaty is a demonstration of what the world can do when we come together in alignment. People said this treaty would never happen. Then they said it would never be ratified. And now it's in force and just last week, another country (joined). So we're now at 60 countries that have ratified it!"

She said there is, "a growing movement in the nuclear space for divestment, from the banks that fund the nuclear weapons producers. When you do the research, you discover that the biggest offender banks funding nuclear weapons are, many of them, the same ones funding fossil fuels. And we know that there's a divestment movement in the climate justice movement. So I am calling for bringing our movements together and for massive divestment... We're seeing who's profiting from this war in Ukraine. It's the arms dealers and it's the fossil fuel providers' companies. So there is a huge obvious intersection here."

In his closing, Richard Falk said, "The Ukraine crisis has generated the most serious danger of escalation close to or over the nuclear threshold since the Cuban missile crisis, in 1962. And it's a moment when... all citizens of conscience should awaken to the dangers, not only that Russia is causing, but that our own government is contributing to."

At the end, I noted that Lazaroff had been taking part with us from Hawai'i, where it was still early morning and occasionally we could all hear roosters crowing in the farmland behind her. I suggested they provided "a wake-up call for all of us!"

Nuclear weapons, nuclear alliances and the costs of militarism

Tom Unterrainer

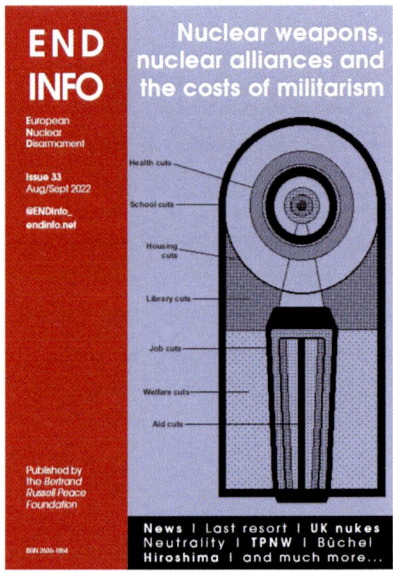

The Stockholm International Peace Research Institute estimates that in 2021, Russian military spending stood at $66,000,000,000 ($66 billion). In the same year the United States spent approximately $801bn. Over the same period, NATO member states, excluding the US, spent $363bn. As Simon Kuper pointed out in the *Financial Times* (9/10 July 2022): "If the US abandons Europe after 2024" - that is, if Trump or one of his protege's wins the Presidential election that year - "other NATO states would outspend Russia more than sixfold."

At the recent NATO conference in Madrid, Secretary-General Stoltenberg announced that the nuclear-armed alliance's 'high-readiness forces' will increase in number from 40,000 to 300,000 by 2023. This is an almost eightfold increase and will include:

> battlegroups in the eastern part of the alliance ... enhanced up to brigade levels, with forces pre-assigned to specific locations; and more heavy weapons, logistics and command-and control assets ... pre-positioned.
> *(Dr. Ian Davis, NATO Watch Briefing Paper No. 96)*

In addition to the upgrade of units and material, President Biden has promised further troop and weapon deployments in Europe and a new HQ in Poland.

The content and implications of NATO's new 'Strategic Concept' will be considered later but suffice to say that the global ambitions, spending commitments, reasserted role of nuclear weapons and the overall posture paint a deadly picture.

NATO is remilitarising and in so doing, enormous damage will be done to rational concepts of peace, security, investment, social security and the environment. Simon Kuper (ibid) quotes Dan Plesch of SOAS, University of London, on the implications of this new wave of militarisation. Plesch warns:

Worst case is we stumble into unintended global war. Best case is we stockpile and never use the weapons, but use our scarce resources on them.

Plesch's warning of "unintended global war" should not be taken lightly and we should not forget what the dimensions of such a war would encompass: the risk of all-out nuclear war and the subsequent destruction of humanity.

In his opening comments to the much-delayed Review Conference of the Non-Proliferation Treaty, UN Secretary-General António Guterres warned that "humanity is just one misunderstanding, one miscalculation away from nuclear annihilation". In subsequent comments, he explained that relying on "luck" - which has stood in the way of such annihilation on more than one occasion - is not a strategy for human survival.

The sharpening tensions arising from Putin's invasion of Ukraine - including stark nuclear tensions - put us all at risk. Yet the response of NATO is unlikely to reduce the tensions, nuclear or otherwise. In fact, such responses follow a pattern we have seen in the past and will undoubtedly replicate the worst possible consequences.

Spend, spend, spend

The New York Times of December 8, 1987 reported that the sum total of United States missiles, aircraft and submarines capable of 'delivering' so-called 'strategic' nuclear warheads amounted to 11,786. The targets for these weapons were 220 urban industrial centres across the Soviet bloc. As Seymour Melman points out in *The Demilitarized Society*: "Hence, US forces have more than fifty times overkill capability."

Melman notes that if this "overkill capability" was reduced by 75%, a budget saving of $54.6 billion ($142 billion in 2022) would be made. Such a reduction would have left the US with an "overkill capability" of twelve. *The Demilitarized Society* (1988) focuses on the problems arising from sustained and extreme levels of military spending in the post-WWII US economy. He explains that whilst money, skill and effort were poured into creating machines of mass annihilation:

> The US now lacks a modern rail system, a modern highway system in good repair ... The city streets are poorly paved. Between a fifth to a third of the highway bridges in the US are rated as needing major repair. Decent housing is no longer available for millions. There is a growth of homelessness and hunger ... Important parts of the population draw water from aquifers that are contaminated. The national parks are in poor repair. The libraries are poorly operated. Waste disposal systems

violate modern technical standards. The public school buildings of New York City require an expenditure of $8 billion for decent repair.

Between 2002 and 2016, the top 100 weapons manufacturers and 'military service' companies logged 38% growth in global sales. In 2016, these sales – excluding Chinese companies – amounted to $375 billion, turning $60 billion profit. Between 1998 and 2011, the Pentagon's budget grew in real terms by 91% while defence industry profits quadrupled.

In the 1970s, investment in the 'information technology' sector stood at $17 billion. By 2017, investment in this sector exceeded $700 billion. In the same year, Apple's market capitalisation stood at $730 billion, Google stood at $581 billion, and Microsoft stood at $497 billion. Meanwhile, Exxon Mobile – the highest placed 'industrial' company – had a market capitalisation of $344 billion. By comparison, the arms manufacturer Lockheed Martin had a capitalisation of around $321 billion and Rolls Royce $21 billion at the end of 2017.

Whilst the United States and other countries continue to purchase – and use – vast quantities of 'conventional' weaponry, the extraordinary figures quoted above occurred alongside the unleashing of a 'Fourth Industrial Revolution', powered by significant leaps in capability in computing, robotics, artificial intelligence, biotechnology, 'autonomous' vehicles and the rest. Ever greater sums are being spent on military and policing applications of the 'fruits' of this 'Revolution'. So much so, that the sociologist William I. Robinson (*Race and Class*, 2018) identifies a trend towards what he terms 'militarised accumulation' as a 'major source of state organised profit-making'.

In 1988, Melman warned that:

(M)assive, sustained military spending is, qualitatively, the single most critical factor in the cumulative depletion of the industrial economy. If this is dealt with decisively then the rest can be addressed. If that factor is unattended, then the rest is rendered unmanageable, and a process of continued decline is locked in place.

Such massive, and long-term, patterns of military expenditure and the material consequences on society at large are made, consistently, in the name of 'security'. Each and every bullet, missile, nuclear warhead, bomber, armed drone, submarine, warship and tank is - we are told - there for 'our security'. This militarised approach to 'security' is riddled with contradictions.

Militarised 'security'

Climate change constitutes a serious threat to global security, an immediate risk to our national security and, make no mistake, it will impact how our military defends our country. And so we need to act - and we need to act now.

President Obama, May 2015

The US army is the most highly funded military organisation in human history. It is also the single largest institutional polluter on the planet. Obama's eloquently delivered speeches on the risks associated with climate change morphed from initially wholesome appeals for action to save humanity, to framing the question as a matter of national security. As Nick Buxton points out ('Securing whose future?' *The Spokesman* 134):

> The Pentagon is the world's single largest organisational user of petroleum: one of its jets, the B-52 Stratocruiser, consumes roughly 3,334 gallons per hour, about as much fuel as the average driver uses in seven years.

As state level reaction to climate catastrophe incorporates more militarised 'security' responses and as multinational efforts at climate change reduction - such as the recent COP26 - fail to meet needs and expectations, it seems likely that militarised responses will be emphasised above other forms. After all, it is much easier to secure funding for military expenditure than for anything else and such expenditure drives corporate profiteering:

> US defence contractor Raytheon openly proclaims its 'expanded business opportunities' arising from 'security concerns and their possible consequences', due to the 'effects of climate change' in the form of 'storms, droughts, and floods'. (Buxton)

Neta Crawford from the 'Costs of War Project' at Brown University estimates that in 2017 alone, the US military emitted more carbon dioxide than Sweden, Denmark and Finland combined (Jessica Fort and Philipp Straub, 'The Carbon Boot-Print', *The Spokesman* 144). Freedom of Information Act (US) requests to the US Defense Logistics Agency, which is responsible for managing fuel purchase and distribution show that in 2017, the Department of Defense emitted 59 million metric tons of carbon dioxide and that from 2001 to 2017, a total of 1,212 million metric tons of the same gas was emitted. These figures include the period covering the bombing, invasion and occupation of Afghanistan and the illegal war against and occupation of Iraq.

Not only do wars, the preparations for war and militarised

responses to 'security' risks have immediate destructive consequences in terms of death, depletion of resources and environmental damage: each and every day that sophisticated and expansive capabilites, such as those embodied in the US military, operate means additional releases of greenhouse gasses into the atmosphere. The impact of US and allied military operations in Iraq could be seen on the TV screen. Civilians on the streets of Baghdad and elsewhere saw the death and catastrophe first hand. What was not reported or broadcast and what has gone largely unmentioned is the legacy of environmental harm arising from these events.

How many B-52s flew in the years of war and occupation? How many hours in total were they in the air? How many gallons does that amount to? How many cubic tons of greenhouse gasses? How many more fractions of a degree did this take us to catastrophic temperature increases? What militarised responses have been put in place to ensure 'security' as a consequence of this increase in temperature? How many B-52s will it take to ensure 'security' from the consequences of war?...

This is just one example of the contradictions that arise in militarised responses to 'security'. In common with other examples, it shares the features outlined earlier: the enormous sums of money devoted to military spending and the way in which such spending shapes the economy more generally. This example also shares another, connected, feature with other militarised responses to 'security': the fact that such responses simply make matters worse.

Law of the instrument

In his *The Psychology of Science* (1966), Abraham Maslow made the following observation:

> I remember seeing an elaborate and complicated automatic washing machine for automobiles that did a beautiful job of washing them. But it could do only that, and everything else that got into its clutches was treated as if were an automobile to be washed. I suppose it is tempting, if the only tool you have is a hammer, to treat everything as if it were a nail.

Whatever else you might think of Maslow's psychological theories, this observation - an outline of the 'Law of the Instrument' - seems a close fit to NATO's approach to 'security'. The nuclear-armed alliance is on the hunt for nails.

However, the fact that NATO is armed to the teeth with hammers is not a sufficient explanation for why it sees every problem as a nail. The purely military-industrial aspect of militarisation might indicate how NATO will react in any given circumstance but it does not account for the US-dominated, nuclear-armed alliance's wider aims and perspectives.

The preface to the 2022 document explains:

> The Strategic Concept emphasises that ensuring our national and collective resilience is critical to all our core tasks and underpins our efforts to safeguard our nations, societies and shared values ...
>
> Our vision is clear: we want to live in a world where sovereignty, territorial integrity, human rights and international law are respected and where each country can choose its own path, free from aggression, coercion or subversion. We work with all who share these goals. We stand together, as Allies, to defend our freedom and contribute to a more peaceful world.

Fine sentiments. Yet the reality of NATO's actions, historic and contemporary, and the belligerence of certain NATO members today, exposes these sentiments as insincere waffle. NATO's new Strategic Concept actually reflects Jens Stoltenberg's perception - and we should assume he largely acts to telegraph the views of the US, in particular - that "we now face an era of strategic competition".

Whereas the 2010 Strategic Concept could proclaim that "the Euro-Atlantic area is at peace and the threat of a conventional attack against NATO territory is low", the 2022 version warns: "the Euro-Atlantic area is not at peace ... We cannot discount the possibility of an attack against Allies." Russia is "the most significant and direct threat to Allies' security and to peace and stability in the Euro-Atlantic area". China is a "systemic challenge" and China's "stated ambitions and coercive policies challenge our interests and values." Russian/Chinese relations are a "deepening strategic partnership".

In the same way that President Bush Jnr concocted an 'Axis of Evil' to mobilise support for his wars of aggression, NATO has now outlined a new 'Axis' of threat, systematically aiming to link Russia and China. All the better for attempting to justify NATO's tilt to China - some distance away from the North Atlantic area! In response, China's mission to the European Union stated:

> NATO's so-called Strategic Concept, filled with cold war thinking and ideological bias, is maliciously attacking China. We firmly oppose it.

We previously argued that US foreign policy under the Trump administration reflected wild and reckless attempts to maintain US influence in a period of shift from unipolarity to multipolarity ('Global Tinderbox', *The Spokesman* 141). The 'bonfire of treaties', aggressive statements and Trump's Nuclear Posture Review reflected these attempts. At the time, Trump could not take NATO with him and devoted some energy to attacking the nuclear-armed alliance, not least for member states reluctance to meet spending commitments.

Trump is no longer the US President, but NATO is now spending positively Trumpian amounts of money on armaments and rearmament. NATO has also fallen into line with US concerns about the emergence of alternative centres of power and influence. This is why they were happy to sign up to the new Strategic Concept and why 'partners' from Australia, Japan, New Zealand and South Korea were welcomed in Madrid.

A nuclear-armed alliance

The strategic nuclear forces of the Alliance, particularly those of the United States, are the supreme guarantee of the security of the Alliance ... NATO's nuclear deterrence posture also relies on the United States' nuclear weapons forward-deployed in Europe and the contributions of Allies concerned.
NATO 2022 Strategic Concept

If, for NATO, every problem is a nail, then the biggest hammer at its disposal is the nuclear weapon. As the Strategic Concept makes clear, it is the "supreme guarantee" of 'security'. Only a truly sick mind could confuse a world-ending weapon of genocide withanything of the sort, but this is the reality we are dealing with.

The expansion of NATO's nuclear bootprint across Europe (see *END Info* 32) and the steady incorporation of Australia, Japan, New Zealand and South Korea into NATO's strategic thinking (see *END Info* 27 for analysis of AUKUS) are conceived of as 'security measures'. These measures, along with massive increases in military spending and troop deployments, sow the seeds of potentially catastrophic outcomes. The catastrophe could be immanent, medium- or long-term, as risks multiply and as pressing concerns around climate change, hunger, pandemic and health intensify.

A truly secure future must mean working for peaceful outcomes to these challenges, not preparing for war.

UK nuclear weapons modernisation update

Dr Tim Street, Nuclear Information Service

The following article first appeared on 28/06/2022 as 'An update on UK nuclear weapons modernisation' on the Nuclear Information Service website (nuclearinfo.org). It is reproduced here with permission of the author.

This article is adapted from a talk given at the 2022 Student and Young Pugwash conference. It gives an overview of the costs and risks involved in the UK nuclear weapons modernisation programme. It also summarises recent research from Nuclear Information Service (NIS), and draws on the work of Peter Burt and Claire Mills.

NIS has estimated the total cost of replacing the UK's nuclear weapon system between 2019 and 2070 to be at least £172bn. It is a huge, national, multi-decade endeavour, with all four elements of the system being replaced. This includes the submarine, missile, warhead, and Infrastructure.

The 2015 Strategic Defence and Security Review described building four new nuclear-armed submarines alone as "equivalent in scale to Crossrail or High Speed 2". However, the UK Government's centre of expertise for major projects has, for several years, warned that the nuclear enterprise is facing serious difficulties. The Infrastructure and Projects Authority's last annual report stated that there had been no improvement in the status of the nuclear projects it reviewed over the previous year.

This article will discuss each element of this vexed programme in turn, beginning with the submarines.

Submarines

Jon Thompson, former permanent secretary at the Ministry of Defence, was asked by MPs in 2015 which project troubled him most. He answered unambiguously: the new nuclear submarines. "The project is a monster," he said. "It keeps me awake at night", because it is the "single biggest future financial risk we face".

Building four new submarines is the most expensive of the UK's nuclear weapons projects. Parliament initially voted to begin the process of building a replacement for the UK's Vanguard-class submarines in 2007. Work on the submarine programme, named Dreadnought, began in March that year.

At that point the first of the four new submarines were supposed to come into service from 2024. The estimated total cost of the project was £15–20bn. The programme moved into its delivery phase in July 2016 following a parliamentary vote.

As of 2022, work is under way on construction of the first two of the four planned new submarines. Procurement of long lead items for the last two submarines has also commenced. The first submarine is now expected to come into service in the early 2030s and will retire in the 2060s. The second delivery phase for Dreadnought was extended by a year due to the Covid-19 pandemic. At present the estimated total cost of the project has gone up to £31bn with a £10bn contingency.

The Dreadnought class will draw upon US submarine designs, so efforts have been made to bring the two nation's replacement programmes in line. For example, the Dreadnought submarines will be powered by a new reactor design, the PWR3, which stands for pressurised water reactor.

The PWR3 is based on a US submarine reactor design and will run on Highly Enriched Uranium fuel. The reactors will be built at Rolls-Royce's Raynesway factory in Derby. However, the company is struggling to upgrade the facilities which are needed to build the PWR3. In addition, the Government's 2021 Defence Equipment plan stated that the manufacture of new reactor cores has been delayed by a year.

It is also important to appreciate that production of the UK's nuclear weapons submarines is connected to production of the UK's hunter killer submarines—known as Astute. All of the seven Astute submarines have faced severe delays, which contribute to the rising costs and risks of building Dreadnought.

Looking more widely, Professor Andy Stirling and Dr Phil Johnstone have highlighted how the UK's nuclear weapons programme depends on civil nuclear energy production. This is because, they explain, the UK's nuclear weapons infrastructure "relies on particular kinds of design expertise, engineering skills, supply chains and regulatory capabilities". Calculating the true cost of the UK being a nuclear weapon state likely therefore requires us to include expenditure in the civil nuclear realm.

There are several other issues which impact on the UK's ability to sustain its nuclear posture. These include: significantly extending the service life of the Vanguard class submarine; a fuel element breach issue in the PWR2 reactor design; and dock capacity at Devonport. These issues, and the way they interact with delays in the Submarine Dismantling Project, could jeopardise the Royal Navy's ability to maintain constant nuclear submarine patrols, known as continuous at sea deterrence.

Missile

The UK's nuclear warheads are delivered by Trident D5 missiles. These are US ballistic missiles to which the UK has access to a common pool. Previously, up to eight operational missiles were deployed on each of the UK's Vanguard submarines. However, following the Government's Integrated Review, published in March 2021, figures on the UK's "operational stockpile, deployed warhead or deployed missile numbers" will no longer be made public, meaning that such numbers may rise.

The life extended version of the D5 missile began to be brought into service in 2017. There is scheduled to be a further life extension, which will last around twenty years, passing through concept, design and deployment phases. A review of this upgraded missile is expected in 2025, followed by ground testing and a first test flight in 2032, before early production begins.

These second life-extend version D5 missiles are set to be loaded onto UK Dreadnought submarines in the late 2030s. This is several years after the first of this now class of submarines comes into service. The focus of the life-extension programme is on developing technologies including: a post-boost control system; guidance instruments; radiation-hardened electronics; battery technologies; and cyber-security frameworks.

The missile compartment of the UK's new Dreadnought submarines will be identical with the US's own new Columbia-class submarines. The UK has paid for a significant proportion of the compartment's development costs. This was because it was expected that the Dreadnought submarines would come into service ahead of the Columbia class, although this now appears unlikely.

Warhead

In February 2020, US officials revealed the existence of a UK replacement warhead programme, which the British Government subsequently confirmed to parliament. The US disclosure led to accusations that the decision was taken without an official UK announcement or appropriate scrutiny. The Integrated Review included an announcement that the UK's warhead stockpile cap would increase from under 225 to 260.

Given these concerning and retrograde developments, NIS is focusing on the UK's next generation warhead. An In-depth analysis of this topic will be provided in a forthcoming report from NIS, currently being written by David Cullen.

Replacement of the UK's current Holbrook warhead (with an upgraded Mk4A version) is thought to have begun in 2016. Monitoring group Nukewatch believe that the three Vanguard class submarines currently available for operational deployment have now been loaded with Mk4A warheads.

As with previous UK warheads, this upgrade is based on a US design. The Mk4A upgrade extends the life of the Holbrook warhead by around 30 years, meaning that it will remain in service until the late 2030s or early 2040s.

The Mk4A was designed as a staging post on the way to a full replacement warhead. New components in the Mk4A include the arming, fusing and firing system, the gas transfer system and new high explosives. The updated fuse allows more precision over the altitude of detonation and the accuracy of the weapon overall has been increased, making it more effective against hardened targets.

The Mk4A upgrade to the UK warhead is part of a wider project called the Nuclear Warhead Capability Sustainment Programme. The programme began in April 2008 and is due to run until April 2025. The total cost of the programme is currently projected to be around £20 billion. Along with the upgrade, this put in place infrastructure deemed necessary for the replacement warhead programme.

The UK's replacement warhead is highly likely to be close in design to the US's new W93 warhead. In addition, the contents of the US's 2018 Nuclear Posture Review and the UK's 2021 Integrated Review suggest that the UK's new warhead will feature improved capabilities.

The UK Government has refused to give information about the timeline of the project citing national security, and has also not revealed details about its cost. However, based on previous timetables and estimates, it would seem that the replacement warhead is intended to come into service around the late 2030s or early 2040s. Regarding cost of the new warhead meanwhile, the BBC estimate this could be around £10 billion over the next 15 years, a figure similar to that previously estimated by NIS.

Much of the UK's infrastructure for deploying, developing and building nuclear weapons is being rebuilt or refurbished. However, the UK's Atomic Weapons Establishment, known as AWE, seems to exist in a state of near constant crisis.

In September 2020 AWE, previously operated as a government owned, commercially operated enterprise, was brought back into public ownership, owing to its poor performance record. Later that year the Chief Nuclear Inspector predicted that AWE Aldermaston would remain under enhanced regulatory attention until at least 2022 because of safety concerns. Most recently, labour disputes and the impact of Covid may have caused further delays to production.

In March 2021 the Ministry of Defence approved funding to restart the troubled Project Pegasus. This project involves building a new enriched uranium manufacturing facility at AWE Aldermaston. Work on the project had been paused over six years ago due to mismanagement, delays and cost overruns. The original project budget for the facility was £634 million, which the MOD are now very likely to exceed.

Several of the infrastructure projects the UK is engaged in relate to the techniques used for nuclear weapons development, in place of live explosive testing. For example, Project Mensa, which involves the construction of a new warhead assembly facility at AWE Burghfield, was approved a month before Pegasus. However, Mensa is delayed by six years and forecast to cost over £1bn more than its original budget. New joint Anglo-French hydrodynamic research facilities for warhead research work are also under construction in France under Project Teutates.

Other infrastructure being modernised includes:

Upgrades to the Trident submarine base at the Clyde Naval Base, which will cost £1.5 billion over the next ten years.

The construction of new facilities at the BAE Systems shipyard at Barrow-in-Furness where the Dreadnought submarines will be built. This is set to cost £300 million.

The construction of a new Core Production facility at Rolls-Royce's Derby factory, where PWR3 reactor components will be produced. Around £1.8 billion has been allocated to this.

Concluding thoughts

Many projects within the UK's nuclear weapons programme have gone vastly over their original budgets. New funding is being poured in to pay for the many projects within the programme facing cost increases.

The programme is also facing severe delays, raising serious questions about the UK's ability to produce this weapons system. Such mounting pressures should be being thrown into sharp relief by developments elsewhere.

For example, the Treaty on the Prohibition of Nuclear Weapons has entered into force. Yet the UK did not participate in negotiations on the treaty and categorically stated that it will not sign or ratify it.

The Covid-19 pandemic has had a devastating impact on communities worldwide. Yet the UK is doubling down on military spending rather than prioritising a green recovery, or supporting a global peace dividend, as recently proposed by leading scientists.

As a party to the Nuclear Non-Proliferation Treaty the UK is committed to reducing the number of its nuclear weapons, and reducing their role in its security policies, pursuant to disarmament. Yet as the 2022 NPT Review Conference approaches, the story the UK has to tell is one of rearmament.

Much greater public and parliamentary scrutiny of the UK's nuclear programme and wider militarisation is therefore needed. This is vital if there is to be any chance of the UK prioritising arms control, non-proliferation and disarmament.

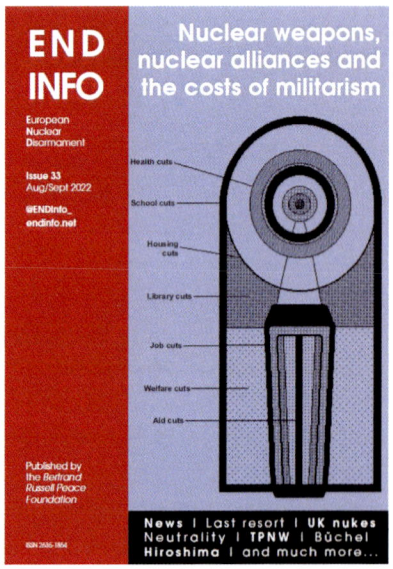

Subscribe to *END Info*

To be added to the email distribution list or to discuss how to receive printed copies of the newsletter, contact **tomunterrainer@russfound.org**
To read previous issues of *END Info* visit **www.spokesmanbooks.org**
Visit **www.endinfo.net** for web-based versions of recent articles.